ABANDON SHIP!

A SURVIVOR'S STORY: THE ATTACK ON PEARL HARBOR, THE SINKING OF THE USS HELENA, SEVEN ADDITIONAL NAVAL BATTLES AND MY LIFE DURING WORLD WAR II

BILL JIM DAVIS

IUNIVERSE, INC.
NEW YORK   BLOOMINGTON

Abandon Ship!
A Survivor's Story: The Attack on Pearl Harbor,
The Sinking of the USS Helena, Seven Additional
Naval Battles and My Life During World War II

iUniverse books may be ordered through booksellers or by contacting:

*iUniverse
1663 Liberty Drive
Bloomington, IN 47403
www.iuniverse.com
1-800-Authors (1-800-288-4677)*

*Because of the dynamic nature of the Internet, any Web addresses or
links contained in this book may have changed since publication and may
no longer be valid.*

*ISBN: 978-1-4401-28950 (pbk)
ISBN: 978-1-4401-28967 (ebk)*

Printed in the United States of America

iUniverse rev. date: 12/2/2009

PRAISE FOR *ABANDON SHIP!*

"Abandon Ship is a fascinating account of enlisted life onboard U.S. naval warships in the Pacific Theater during WWII. It is an honest and frank account of one who traveled in harm's way for the duration of the war and survived. We, as a nation, are forever indebted to the young Davis and countless others like him who answered the call to duty and performed with valor. Those young men and women who aspire to service in the United States Navy would be well served by reading this book."

Michael Stimson
CDR, JAGC, USN (ret)

"You wrote in such a way that I believed I was there with you, seeing all the action and feeling all the emotions. How fortunate that this fascinating history has been preserved in such a unique way. It was interesting, exciting, and enthralling!"

Martha B. Brasfield
Chancellor - 25th Judicial District
State of Tennessee

"I very much enjoyed reading your WWII memoir Abandon Ship! Thank you for your service to our country and to this community. Your fidelity in public duty and your example of unselfish dedication is one that speaks volumes to those who come behind you. Thank you for sharing your story."

J. Houston Gordon
Author and Prominent Attorney
Covington, Tennessee

PREFACE...

Life is filled with experiences of one kind or another with only a few having a major impact upon our lives.

During my lifetime four experiences stand-out above the others. Marriage to Jean in 1946 & Helen in 1994 proved to be the best decisions I ever made. Becoming an Agent for State Farm Insurance Companies has provided both challenging and rewarding work opportunities. Campaigning for the US Congress in 1969 followed by my election in 1970 and re-election to 3 four year terms in the Tennessee State Senate, made me aware of the awesome power we place in the hands of a few at all levels of government. Based upon my observations inside the system, it is a miracle our system of government has survived over 200 years of political abuse.

The fourth and by far the most hazardous and action packed period of my life were the seven years I served in the Navy from December 1938 to February 1946. This tour of duty spanned 3 peace-time years and 4 wartime years...World War II from beginning to end.

My Navy years are what this book is all about. These experiences are not unique. Thousands upon thousands of Navy men could tell a similar story. It is my purpose to relive those years giving the reader a sense of Navy life during this period. In particular the war in the Pacific as we pushed the Japanese back across the Pacific from Pearl Harbor to Tokyo.

Bill Jim Davis

CONTENTS

LIFE BEFORE NAVY YEARS..

I was born in Memphis, Tennessee on August 31, 1920. Nine years later, when the Great Depression hit, my dad lost his job with the railroad and the family moved 40 miles North to a small rural community, called Charleston, located in Tipton County approximately 10 miles from Covington on the highway to Stanton.

Charleston was typical of the thousands of farming communities located throughout the South during the period. In the center of the community were 2 churches, 2 grocery stores, a grammar school, cotton gin, and blacksmith shop & grist mill. Within 18 months after our arrival, dad opened his own grocery store giving the community 3 grocery outlets.

From opening day my brother Roy (born in 1922) and I spent most of our spare time at the store. In the beginning we were more of a nuisance than help. However, by the time we reached High School dad began to depend more and more on our work at the store. By then he had purchased a 100-acre farm nearby and spent much of his time there. He would leave us in charge for hours at a time and each summer for several days while he and mother were away on vacation-usually visiting mother's relatives in Texas.

I should mention that two sisters were added to the family during the early 1930's... Joy in 1931 and Shirley in 1933.

Roy and I were luckier than most boys our age. Our friends had to work in their fathers' cotton and corn fields from sunup to sundown. It wasn't a matter of choice, rather one of survival in those depression years. Farm families from the youngest to the oldest had to work in the fields just to feed and clothe the family.

Although we were never paid for our work in the store, there was what we considered adequate compensation. Dad would arrange for us to see a double feature movie at the Ruffin Theatre in Covington each Saturday afternoon.

In addition to our work in the store, we had chores to do around the house. My principle responsibility, and the one I disliked the most, was milking the family cow. Bessie had to be milked twice a day regardless of weather conditions or activities I had planned for the day. Roy was smart; he avoided learning how to milk Bessie like the plague. When 1938 rolled around, I was seventeen and in my final year in high school.

ON THE WORLD SCENE DURING 1938: Germany occupied Austria and parts of Czechoslovakia setting the stage for World War II.

ON THE HOME FRONT DURING 1938: Our Nation continued to be mired in the worst depression in our history. Farm hands were earning 50 cents a day when they could find work. Those working off the farm didn't fare much better. Congress adopted a new wages and hour law, setting 40 cents an hour minimum wage for manufacturing jobs with a maximum work week of 44 hours.

Possibly as a consequence of the hard times, the moral fiber of our nation was never stronger. Churches had a profound impact upon our laws and every aspect of community life. Few objected to "Blue Laws" that brought business activities to a virtual stand-still on Sunday's, as Americans, young and old alike, filled churches to overflow for morning & evening services.

We were poor. Everyone was poor... By today's standards over 90% of the citizens of Tipton County would have been on Welfare. The truly needy were helped by the community-neighbor helped neighbor-very few, even those in dire circumstances, had too much pride to ask for public assistance.

Visiting neighbors, listening to a battery-powered radio, and attending an occasional movie were the principal sources of relaxation and entertainment in those days. Our family never missed Lum & Abner, Amos & Andy, or Jack Benny on radio. Every one with 25 cents went to see Walt Disney's first full-length movie, "SNOW WHITE & THE SEVEN DWARFS".

The people may have been miserable inside, but outwardly they were happy and carefree. I heard more folks singing and whistling in those days than at any time since. Whistling was especially popular in 1938, following the release of the Disney movie featuring a hit song, "WHISTLE WHILE YOU WORK".

The depression didn't dampen the patriotic spirit among Americans. Kate Smith, one of the top vocalists of the day, revived a 1917 song written by Irving Berlin, and made "GOD BLESS AMERICA" almost our national anthem. Only a few blamed the government for the depression. There were no riots or demonstrations. I shudder to think what would happen in this country if a similar recession hit today.

BACK TO MY STORY: With my High School years fast coming to a close, I had a decision to make: What to do with my life following graduation? I thought about college, but college was not a viable option for two reasons: tuition and other expenses would strain the family's limited resources plus attending college without the foggiest idea what profession I wanted to follow later in life just didn't make sense.

Another option was working full-time in the family store. Dad had even mentioned the possibility of a partnership later on. The work was relatively easy and the pay would have been better than farming, but working 10 to 12 hours a day, 6 days a week, seemed no life at all even if the partnership became a reality.

The truth was, I wanted to get away from home. I wanted adventure, something different that would give me an opportunity to make a decision about my future. This was the reason a Navy poster "JOIN THE NAVY & SEE THE WORLD" was so enticing.

It was even more appealing because my father had often talked about his experiences aboard the battleship *U.S.S. Nevada* during World War I. Four years in the Navy would give me plenty of time to consider other options.

Navy recruiting personnel didn't have to recruit me, I recruited them! In April I went by the Navy recruiting office located in the Main Post Office on Front Street in Memphis and signed up for a 4-year tour of duty. At the time the Navy was only accepting 3 or 4 new recruits each month from the Memphis area so my name was placed on a waiting list. I was told it would probably be October or November before I would receive orders to report for active duty.

During the summer months that followed I worked for the US Department of Agriculture mapping farm land. In exchange for government price support, farmers were allocated a specific number of acres of cotton to cultivate. I was part of a crew of men, virtually all high school graduates, hired temporarily to measure the cotton acreage on each farm to make sure the farmer didn't over plant. The pay was exceptionally good for the times... $5.00 per day and car expenses.

When the mapping program ended in August, I began working full-time in the family grocery store. Waiting to be called-up by the Navy was tough. Now that the decision had been made to join the Navy, I wanted to get on with this phase of my life-the sooner the better.

Although I checked with the Recruiting Office in September, October, and again in November, it was early

December before orders arrived to report for duty. On December 13, 1938 in Nashville, Tennessee, I was formerly sworn-in. When 1939 arrived, I was in the early stages of recruit training at the Naval Training Station, Norfolk, Virginia.

ON THE WORLD SCENE IN 1939: Most Americans were too busy trying to survive during those Depression Years to notice the world was moving closer & closer to World War II. On September 1, 1939 Germany invaded Poland. Two days later England & France declared war on Germany signaling the beginning of the worst Holocaust in World history.

ON THE HOME FRONT IN 1939: The New York World's Fair reopened on April 30 with opening ceremonies telecast over NBC's experimental TV channel. It was another great year for movies: "GONE WITH THE WIND" & "THE WIZARD OF OZ"...two all-time classics...were released that year. Superman, Buck Rogers, and Batman comic books were popular with the kids. Glenn Miller became the #1 band leader in the country. Little league baseball & paperback books were introduced that year. Several top songs of the year: OVER THE RAINBOW (song from the OZ movie), DEEP PURPLE, SOUTH OF THE BORDER, WISHING, SCATTER BRAIN & JEEPERS CREEPERS.

PEACE TIME NAVY: 1939-1941

I liked military life from the beginning. I liked the uniforms, inspections, regimentation, and food, everything including the salary which was $21 per month!

I'm quite sure I was no more than the average recruit. It was a learning and adjusting experience. The principle lesson learned--follow orders to the letter and ask questions later.

At the end of recruit training (March 1939), I was automatically promoted to Seaman 2nd class. The promotion added another stripe to my uniform and increased my pay to $36 per month.

Two weeks before the close of Recruit Training, all recruits were tested to determine if they qualified for specialized training. My test scores made me eligible to attend a 21-week Machinist course. Since the school was located at the training center, it was only necessary to move my living quarters a few barracks away from the recruit area.

I soon discovered the life of a Navy student was entirely different from that of a recruit. The extra stripe on my sleeve and moving out of the Recruit training area meant more freedom and fewer restrictions on my day-to-day activities. We continued to march to classes, but otherwise free to come and go around the base as we pleased. Three week-ends out of four we could go ashore on liberty. One week-end each month we had to stay aboard for guard duty around the barracks and school area.

Each Saturday every student with a week-end pass would head for the Base entrance for a street car ride to downtown Norfolk some 10 miles from the Base. It was apparent from my first week-end ashore that Navy men in uniform had a terrible reputation among the civilian population. One sailor reported (never confirmed) seeing a sign at a city park that read, "DOGS & SAILORS NOT ALLOWED". It was easy to understand why the bad reputation. A few (a very small percentage-usually ship-based sailors) would spend their liberties ashore in the bar and brothel area of the city. Too often their liberties would become little more than drunken orgies with a number being hauled away in the wee hours of the morning. by Navy Shore Patrol or local police.

As always, it is the low morals of the 2 or 3 percent of an organization that determines the reputation of the entire group. Virtually all of the permanently based Navy personnel (which numbered several hundred at the time) were married and living off base with their families. They were law-abiding, civic-minded, and solid citizens of the community. They, too, were stained with the same bad reputation.

All of the student (& recruit) population had to wear uniforms ashore. A few would change into civilian clothes at the YMCA just as soon as they arrived in downtown Norfolk to conceal their Navy ties. The rest of us were considered, on sight, as part of the group that frequented the shady sections of the city.

Consequently, students would go ashore in groups of two, three, or four, attend a movie-sometimes two…have dinner in a nice restaurant…then return to the base. On occasions, we would go to Virginia Beach for a swim in the ocean, and return to the base by 10 to 11 at night. Some would stay over on Saturday night for a dance at the YMCA which was about the only contact we had with girls our age. Parents would usually not permit their daughters to date a sailor in uniform.

My leisure time on duty weekends were spent doing school homework, listening to the radio, and going to a movie (shown at the Base Theatre each night). On occasions, I would attend a movie aboard one of the ships tied-up at a pier less than a mile from our barracks.

I was captivated by Navy Ships, especially those with big guns, Destroyers, Cruisers, and Battleships. There were always 6 to 10 ships of various types tied up near the Training Center. On Sunday afternoons, I would go aboard at least one, sometimes two, just to talk to members of the crew and look around.

During the last two weeks of Machinist training, the world's attention was focused on Europe. Germany was demanding return of territory given to Poland following World War I. When their demands were not resolved peacefully, Germany invaded Poland. The entire world would soon be at war!

After a two-week leave at home, following graduation from Machinist School, I returned to Norfolk for re-assignment to a permanent duty station or ship. I had requested a combat ship. I definitely did not want shore duty or a service type ship, a supply, tanker, repair, or similar type vessel. I wanted a ship with big guns on it. I wanted a ship that would likely be in the thick of battle should the United States become involved in the war in Europe.

I wasn't disappointed. I was ordered to report to the *U.S.S. Helena*, a "light cruiser" located at the Brooklyn Navy Yard in New York. The *Helena* was a new ship…commissioned on September 18, 1939, and a fighting ship! I reported 3 days after the *Helena* was commissioned thereby not classified as a "plank owner" (a Navy term for those who are on board the day the ship is placed into service).

The basic characteristics of the *Helena* were: Length-600 feet, width at Beam (amidship 61 feet), Displacement (weight) 10,000 tons, top speed-33 knots (about 40 MPH), 15 six-inch guns in 5 turrets (three forward & two aft), and 8 five-inch guns in 4 turrets (two on each side of the ship).

When I reported aboard I expected to be assigned to the Machine Shop in the Engineering Department. Surely they would take advantage of the training I received at Norfolk. Wrong! This is one of the many lessons I learned about the Navy. One Chief Petty Officer explained…there is a right way, a wrong way, and the Navy way of doing things.

Regardless of background, education, or training, you were assigned to fill whatever vacancies were available when you reported aboard a new ship or station. Surprisingly the "Navy way" worked. I saw it happen again and again. Men were assigned to positions totally unrelated to their background or training, yet within 6 months would become as effective and efficient as most of those trained for the position.

Since there were no openings in the Machine Shop, I was assigned to the Electrical Division of the Engineering Department. I was now a "striker" (apprentice) electrician.

This is one example of the many decisions made by forces beyond my control that changed the course of my life. These unseen forces play an important role in everyone's life. Some call it fate, but in more instances than we care to admit, it is providence guiding and directing our lives.

Had I been assigned to the Machine Shop, my battle station would most likely have been in an Engine or Boiler Room increasing the odds of being killed or injured at Pearl Harbor and Kula Gulf. It is also very doubtful I would have had the same promotional opportunities as a machinist.

Although the *Helena* was commissioned, she was not ready to join the fleet. There was equipment to be tested, sea trials, and a shake-down cruise before the *Helena* could be assigned to a battle unit. In the meantime, there was plenty of liberty for the crew in New York. I was ashore every minute possible.

New York is a fabulous city. I toured the World's Fair (opened in 1938 and continued through 1939). I visited Grant's tomb, St John's Cathedral, Museum of Natural History, Statue of Liberty, Wall Street, Broadway, and scores of other places. I rode the subway all over New York from one side to the other. I was having a ball!!

I saw several movies and the Rockette's at Radio City Music Hall. Although there were many, I only bought tickets to one stage show: "TOBACCO ROAD". There were several fabulous movie theatres along Broadway. Several were open around the clock. Two or three, the Paramount in particular, would have big name bands, popular comedians (like Red Skelton), or a popular singer (like Frank Sinatra) on stage before the movie.

The Navy gave us tickets to live Radio Broadcasts. I attended several, but can only remember seeing Fred Waring and his band & the Tony Martin show.

While in New York, I was promoted to Fireman First-Class. I was now making $42 per month and spending every dime & more. On one occasion I pawned my wrist watch for $10 cash, just to tide me over until the next pay-day.

In late November we left the Brooklyn Navy Yard for sea trials. The purpose was to test the sea-worthiness of the *Helena*, in particular the main propulsion engines. As it turned out it was a test of the crew as well.

The trials lasted five days. It was a miserable five days for me. Although they didn't classify the weather as stormy, there were 40 to 50 mph winds. We encountered waves 10 to 15 feet high. The *Helena* rolled and tossed like a cork. The maneuvering, testing, and operating at full throttle only made conditions worse.

I was sea-sick almost from the moment we cleared New York Harbor until we sighted the Statue of Liberty on our return. I wasn't the only one sea-sick. All of those who had never been at sea before were sick. Even some of the old-timers were sick as well. Other than a four-hour watch at an electrical switchboard in the Forward Engine Room each 12 hours, I was in my bunk. I never ate a complete meal during the entire trip. The little I did swallow came right back up. This was the first and last time I experienced any problems with sea-sickness during my entire Navy career.

On December 21, 1939, we left New York on a "Shakedown Cruise" to Brazil, Uruguay, and Argentina in South America. All Navy ships have these type cruises shortly after commissioning. In peace-time they are longer and more elaborate than during war-time. Such cruise's are for testing and training, but our primary purpose on this trip was to show the American flag in these South American countries.

On our way south, we stopped at Annapolis, Maryland for cadets at the naval academy to tour the ship. While there, we ushered in a new year...1940.

ON THE WORLD SCENE IN 1940: The war in Europe began to heat-up. Before the year was out, Germany had invaded and captured Belgium, Holland, France, and Denmark. The battle for Great Britain began.

ON THE HOME FRONT IN 1940: A new Selective Service Law was enacted, requiring draft registration of all men 20 to 36. We were becoming more and more involved in the war providing England with equipment and supplies of every description short of war. To underscore our support, we gave England 50 World War I vintage Destroyers to help in their fight against the German submarine menace. Franklin D. Roosevelt was elected President for an unprecedented third term. Nylon stockings made a brief appearance before being diverted to Military use.

On January 3, 1940, we stopped at Guantanamo, Cuba for two days.

Further South near the Equator, I was forced to participate in a most unusual ceremony. Since over 50% of the crew had never been near the Equator before, we were classified as "Pollywogs" and considered unfit to cross the Equator. To qualify we had to be thoroughly "indoctrinated" by King Neptune and his Court. We would then be "Shellbacks" and allowed to cross the Equator. This practice must have been originated by some sadistic creature that enjoyed seeing others suffer.

The fun began when the "Jolly Roger" was hoisted to the foremast signaling the arrival of King Neptune with his Court. Approximately 450 "Pollywogs" were lined-up and forced to walk (no running permitted) through a double-line of "Shellbacks" who tried to beat us to a pulp. Some used wooden paddles and others canvas tubes filled with sawdust soaked in water. I was black and blue for weeks following this ordeal.

After the beating, we were forced to swallow a revolting tasting substance formed into the shape of a pill, about the size & half the length of your little finger. Then we had to kiss the "Royal Baby's" pot-belly. Next the "Royal Barber" butchered our hair. The barber chair was swiveled over the side of a hugh canvas tank filled with salt water. When the barber was through, he pushed the chair back throwing the occupant head-first into the water. Immediately two "Royal Lifeguards" grabbed each victim as they struggled to the surface, telling them to say "Shellback". Before they could respond the "lifeguards" pushed them underwater again. This process was repeated again and again (almost on the verge of drowning) until the victim, on the verge of drowning, was permitted to say "Shellback." Finally, we were forced to crawl through a canvas tunnel filled with a mixture of oil, flour, and lamp black. We were a mess!!

As we continued south, we noticed that the seasons of the year are opposite from those in the States. We left New York in mid-winter. It was mid-summer in Argentina, Uruguay, and Brazil.

We docked in Buenos Aires on January 22. With a population of about three million, Buenos Aires was (and still is, I believe) the largest city in South America. We found people friendly, but we couldn't socialize because they spoke Spanish. In passing, they would look at our uniforms, say a few words in Spanish and smile.

The language barrier didn't pose much of a problem since we spent most of our off-duty hours sight-seeing and eating. We always found one or two at every stop who could speak English.

Their food was bargain priced. A steak dinner with all the trimmings, including wine (served with all lunch and dinner meals) cost one Peso, 25 cents American.

In the beginning we ordered coffee with our meals, but there were very few repeat orders. The coffee they served was unlike anything we had tasted before. We knew there would be a difference when we saw the cups they served the coffee in. They were about 1/3 the size American restaurants use. After tasting the brew, we could understand why. The liquid was as thick as syrup, super hot, with an over-powering coffee taste. We made the mistake of trying to drink it like the coffee they served aboard ship. Their variety had to be sipped slowly.

On our first liberty, we saw scores of German sailors in uniform every place we went. They were survivors of the German Pocket-Battleship *Graf Spee* that had been scuttled just off-shore at Montevideo, Uruguay. They were well-behaved and friendlier than the French and British Sailors we came in contact with.

How they happened to be in this part of the world is an interesting story. From the beginning of WWII, the British had the German fleet bottled up in the North Sea. However, on occasions, a ship would slip through to raid British shipping. One of the most famous was the *Graf Spee.*

The *Graf Spee* had slipped through the British Blockade shortly after the war started. She roamed the seas for months, sinking twenty plus British Merchant Ships, before being cornered by three British Cruisers.

In the battle that followed, all three British ships and the *Graf Spee* were damaged. Had the *Spee* Captain known the extent of damage to the British he would have continued the fight. Instead he broke-off the engagement and docked at Montevideo, Uruguay for supplies, ammunition, and refueling. He had intended to stay in port no more than 48 hours, but local government officials (under pressure from the British) delayed the *Spee* departure four days. The delay gave the British time to assemble more ships in the vicinity, thereby giving them an over-whelming advantage should the German raider leave port.

It was a dramatic moment. The British were patrolling back and forth outside the harbor when the *Graf Spee* got underway heading for the open sea. The *Spee* paused about six miles from shore. The crew could be seen entering life boats and pulling away from the ship. When the life boats were a safe distance away, there was a tremendous explosion and the *Graf Spee* sank. The German Government decided it best to scuttle the ship rather than risk certain destruction by the British. Most of the crew was interned for the duration of the war in Argentina. A week later Captain Langsdorf, skipper of the *Graf Spee*, committed suicide.

We left Buenos Aires on January 29 & arrived in Montevideo, the capital of Uruguay the next day. The city was much like Buenos Aires, only smaller... population around 700,000. The language and currency were the same as in Argentina. There wasn't much sight-seeing there. It started raining the day we arrived and continued most of our stay.

We left Montevideo on February 3 and arrived in Santos, Brazil on February fifth. By now I could speak and understand a few words of Spanish. I expected to be able to better understand Portuguese, the language of Brazil. Not so! Even though I understood a few words of Spanish from the beginning, I never understood a word of Portuguese during our entire stay in Brazil.

At the time Santos was the coffee exporting capital of the world. As we pulled into port, mountains of coffee beans could be seen piled high along the dock waiting to be shipped overseas. Santos was the smallest city we visited, with a population of approximately 175,000.

When we docked, the city was in the middle of their Mardi Gras celebration. I have never visited New Orleans during their Mardi Gras festivities, but, if the Santos variety is any indication, it is wild! I made the mistake of standing curb-side as the carnival parade passed. Many of the marchers carried bottles of cheap perfume which they sprayed freely on spectators along the way. When I returned to the *Helena* my white uniform was a mess and I smelled like a brothel-house madam.

While in Santos, we were given an opportunity to go sightseeing in San Paulo, the second largest city in Brazil, about 50 miles from Santos. The highlight of the trip was the cable car ride up a 2700 foot mountain. Their restaurants, shops, buildings, and movie houses were more like those in the states than any of the other 3 cities we visited. We arrived back in New York on March 2.

I enjoyed the orderly routine of a peace-time Navy. The war in Europe, at this time, seemed too far away for the United States to become an active participant.

I liked electrical work; I studied the courses provided for advancement. At the same time I applied myself to the regimentation of shipboard life and did my work assignments to the best of my ability. It paid off. My superiors recommended me for advancement as soon as I accumulated the required time in grade. During 1940, I was promoted to 3rd Class, then 2nd Class Petty Officer and in the summer of 1941 moved up to first class Petty Officer. With each new step, there was a corresponding increase in pay from $54 to $72 to $84 per month.

We operated off the East Coast for several months following our return from South America. In September we moved through the Panama Canal to the West Coast. After a short stay in San Diego and San Francisco, we joined our Pacific Fleet operating out of Pearl Harbor, Hawaii.

We were tied-up to a pier at Pearl Harbor when the new year-1941-arrived.

MAKING NEWS IN 1941:

Germany captured Hungary, Yugoslavia, Rumania, and Greece which landed troops in North Africa. In June 1941, they invaded Russia. Later in the year, they were thrown back at Leningrad and Moscow.

On December 7, Japanese planes would strike Pearl Harbor. The entire world would be at war. Our nation would never be the same.

ON THE HOME FRONT:

An Atomic Research Program, that resulted in the Atomic Bomb, was started in Chicago. In December, gas and tire rationing began.

As part of the Pacific fleet our routine changed drastically. Instead of moving leisurely from place to place alone, we were now part of a task force being trained to act as a unit. We were at sea about half the time. There were drills of every description, in particular simulated battle maneuvers and gunnery exercises. It was a time of testing of men and equipment. It was a time of training men to become more proficient in the operation and maintenance of the *Helena's* guns and machinery. All of the training & testing would prove invaluable in time of battle or emergency as we would soon discover.

There was plenty of time off for liberty and recreation. On the East Coast, we had liberty in Boston, New York, and Norfolk. On the West Coast, it was Long Beach, San Diego, and San Francisco. In Hawaii, it was Honolulu.

The reputation of a Navy man during this period was not the best. It was easy to understand why. After several days and sometimes weeks at sea, most sailors went ashore to let off steam. The nicer places in town were not interested in this type of clientele. As a result, sailors usually went to the rougher sections of town, where there were frequent fights and drunken brawls.

Most of my older shipmates were married, but they were not always good relationships. There were frequent separations, with the husband in one location and the wife another. Consequently, infidelity by both marriage partners was the rule rather than the exception. I made a pledge not to get married as long as I remained in the Navy.

Navy men are accused of having a "girl in every port". Most do, but too often, they were bar pickups or street girls. As a result, venereal diseases were common among the crew. Many of the older men considered gonorrhea no more harmful than the common cold. This was especially true of those who had contracted the disease several times. One of my Chief Petty Officer's had been treated for gonorrhea seven times and syphilis twice during his twelve years of service.

The Navy had a policy, at the time, of assigning close family members to the same ship or station-if requested. (This policy was changed in November 1943 when the 5 Sullivan brothers lost their lives when their ship was torpedoed and sank in the South Pacific) My brother, Roy, joined the Navy on November 1, 1940. After recruit training, he requested to be assigned to the *Helena* and reported aboard in August,

1941. He was also assigned to the "E" Division which made our relationship even closer.

It was good to have Roy with me. Although we seldom went on liberty together, he was family and home, which helped erase those periods of loneliness & home-sickness that happened from time-to-time.

As the year progressed, everyone's attention was focused more and more on the war in Europe. In addition, we were becoming more and more involved by providing England with supplies and equipment of every description.

While the war in Europe dominated the news, a crisis was developing in the Pacific. Japan had been at war with China since 1937. By 1941 they seemed to be bogged-down in that vast people and land mass as so many other invaders had done in centuries past. During these years we helped their war effort by selling them all the supplies and materials they wanted for their war machine.

However, in the summer of 1941, when Japan announced plans to invade Indochina, the British, the Dutch, and the United States placed an embargo on steel, oil, and other war materials destined for Japan. The leaders of Japan were desperate. They could not continue the war in China much less pursue a conquest of Indochina without oil in particular. They had a decision to make.

Either give up plans to invade Indochina or be prepared to fight the British, the Dutch, and the United States and take the oil they needed, located in the Dutch East Indies. They elected to fight and made their plans accordingly.

Their plan was: strike without warning, destroy our Pacific Fleet based at Pearl Harbor, destroy all American and British air and naval units in the Far East, and then occupy all of the islands in the Pacific. With the entire Pacific (west of Hawaii) under their control, they were certain they could easily negotiate peace to end the war.

Although there were continuing negotiations to end the embargo, until the very day of the attack, the die had been cast. On November 26, 1941, a Japanese task force, built around six aircraft carriers, carrying 423 combat planes, left bases in Japan with orders to strike Pearl Harbor.

The "DAY OF INFAMY" WAS AT HAND!!

WAR YEARS

PEARL HARBOR-DECEMBER 7, 1941

In the weeks preceding that fateful day, units of the Pacific Fleet would routinely go to sea on Monday's for training exercises and return to Pearl Harbor on week-ends for liberty and recreation for their crews.

On this particular week-end, the *Helena* was tied-up alongside a Navy Yard Dock (#10-10) just a few hundred yards across the main channel from Ford Island where seven battleships were moored. The battleship *Pennsylvania* was in Dry Dock less than 200 yards forward of the *Helena*.

There wasn't any warning, alert, or indication on Saturday, December 6, that the Japanese attack was only hours away. Only the title of the movie Saturday night, "Hold Back the Dawn" warned of impending danger. The *Helena* "PLAN OF THE DAY" for Sunday the 7th is copied below:

USS HELENA
PLAN OF THE DAY
SUNDAY 7, DECEMBER 1941

DAILY ROUTINE IN PORT EXCEPT:

DUTY WATCH SECTION 4, WORK DIVISION 2, DUTY
ML NO. 1 MILITARY AND MEDICAL GUARD- USS ST
LOUIS
DUTY HEAD OF DEPARTMENT- LTCDR. BUERKLE

0800   Rig for church on forecastle. Muster on stations.
        Confessions in Library. Shore Patrol leave ship.
0830   Mass on forecastle.

Notes: (a) Annual Material Inspection will be conducted
Monday
8 December 1941. Open all voids, fire control tubes, wiring
passages under turret handling rooms, and have the lower
drawers of desks, transoms and bunks removed.
      (b) Scrub all divisional laundry bags, inside and
outside. (c) Tomorrow December 8, is feast of
Immaculate Conception. (d) Movies for Saturday 6
December 1941

"HOLD BACK THE DAWN" with Charles Boyer, Olivia de
Havilland. Mark 3.9

                  V.C. BARRINGER, Jr.,
                  Commander, U.S. Navy Executive
                  Officer.

      Sunday morning, December 7, 1941, prior to 7:55AM, was
no different than any other Sunday morning we had become
accustomed to while in port. Holiday routine was the order of
the day. One-half of the crew had been given liberty and many
of that group were ashore. The weather was clear, there was a
slight breeze, and the temperature in the 70's.
      Most of the crew were up and about by 7AM. By 7:30, I
had finished breakfast. A few minutes later, I reported to my
mustering station, the Electric Shop, located on the 3rd Deck,

to have my presence recorded. After talking to shipmates for several minutes, I left the shop to go top-side to purchase a Sunday newspaper. There was always a news-boy at the gangway selling the Honolulu Star-Bulletin each Sunday morning. The time was about 7:45 and ten minutes before the first bomb fell on Ford Island.

Everything topside seemed perfectly normal. As usual only a few men were around. Some were reading, some carrying on idle conversation, and others just strolling in the fresh air. Only a handful of men were on duty: no more than three or four below deck in Engineering spaces, less than a half-dozen posted topside near the gangway and signal bridge, and I noticed the Color Guard preparing to make colors at 0800.

After purchasing the Sunday paper, I went below to my living quarters, located 4 decks (floors) down from the main deck, just below the water-line. If there is one place you don't want to be during a torpedo attack, it is below the water-line of any ship. I was standing by my bunk preparing to lie down to read the paper, when the General Alarm sounded. The time was 7:56; one minute after the first bomb fell on Ford Island.

We had been trained to respond to any General Alarm by reporting to our Battle Stations as quickly as possible. But, this was Sunday morning. Never before had we been called upon to report to our Battle Stations on a Sunday morning in port. Sunday was always a day of rest and relaxation for off duty personnel.

We thought it was a drill or someone had accidentally tripped the alarm mechanism. As a consequence, we slowly and reluctantly began to make our way to our Battle Station.

Any questions we had about the sounding of the General Alarm were answered in seconds. I was no more than a few feet from my bunk, when suddenly there was a tremendous explosion, shaking the entire ship, knocking me down. The lights went out. We were in total darkness. The time was

Bill Jim Davis

7:57AM. The time is exact. (a clock in the Forward Engine Room, where the torpedo hit, stopped at this exact moment)

Fear gripped my entire body. I thought a powder magazine had exploded. There was almost panic as we raced to our Battle Stations.

The scene in and around my Battle Station (A Damage Control unit located amid-ship, just below the main deck) was one of mass confusion. Men were coming and going in every direction. Most were heading for their Battle Station, but several had been wounded and were seeking medical attention.

I stopped two of my electrical buddies, who had severe burns around their face, arms, and legs (uniform of the day was short sleeve shirts and short trousers). I asked them what had happened. They didn't know. They only knew they had been hit by a ball of fire in the passageway near the entrance to the Forward Engine Room.

The chaotic situation, coupled with anxiety and fear caused me to leave my post to go topside. Surely, I thought, someone there could tell me what had happened or I could see for myself.

When I reached the main deck, I could see clouds of smoke in every direction. The sound and vibrations of numerous explosions filled the air. I noticed a few planes, but at the moment it didn't register with me that they were responsible for the explosions, smoke and fire. The Battleship *Oklahoma* had already rolled over on its side.

I couldn't believe my eyes. Surely this was some horrible nightmare. For a few moments I was hypnotized by the scene unable to move.

Then a plane no more than 50 yards away, flying at tree-top level, brought me back to reality. I could see every detail of the plane including the pilot. He dipped the wings of his plane slightly as he flew by. The bright red balls on each wing tip were clearly visible. Then it hit me!!

WE WERE BEING ATTACKED BY JAPANESE PLANES!! THE *HELENA* HAD BEEN TORPEDOED!!

WE WERE AT WAR!!

I can only guess the plane I saw was the one that had torpedoed the *Helena*. The pilot was simply taking a closer look at the damage he had done.

There were 191 planes in the first phase of the Japanese attack. Of this number, 40 torpedo planes and 51 dive bombers had orders to destroy our ships and planes at Pearl Harbor. The remaining planes were assigned other targets on the Island.

I recognized the planes as being Japanese no more than 2 or 3 minutes after 8AM. Our guns were silent. The Japanese were having a field day.

The *Helena* had been severely damaged. The torpedo had blasted a hole in the starboard side of the Forward Engine Room. The damaged area was 40 ft long with the hole, at the point of impact, large enough for a man to stand in. The explosion also damaged the bulkhead (wall) between the Forward Engine and Forward Fire Rooms, quickly flooding both compartments. Instantly we were without steam, power, and lights. As fate would have it, the generator supplying electricity and the boiler supply steam were located in these two compartments.

The minelayer *Oglala*, tied up alongside the *Helena* was sinking. Strange as it may seem, no bomb or torpedo actually made contact with the *Oglala*. The torpedo that had damaged the *Helena* passed underneath the much lighter and smaller *Oglala*. The concussion from the explosion of the torpedo against the side of the *Helena* ripped open the hull of the *Oglala*.

Live ammunition was stored in compartments near the ship's bottom, but these spaces were locked. The Gunnery Officer, who had custody of the keys, was ashore on liberty. Ammunition handlers waited only a few moments for the keys to arrive, then using axes and bolt cutters, the padlocks were quickly severed. In less than ten minutes, live ammunition was flowing to our guns topside.

The exact time the *Helena* and other ships opened fire isn't known, but it had to be more than 10 minutes after the attack started. Japanese photographs taken as late as 8:05 show no anti-aircraft fire. The shock and confusion following the initial alarm and explosion of the torpedo lasted only a few minutes. The *Helena* crew was now ready to put their training to the test.

Our task was made easier when electricity was restored within minutes after the torpedo hit the Forward Engine Room. The *Helena* was equipped with two diesel powered electric generators, one forward and the other aft of the flooded compartments. Both were on line, supplying electricity, in less than five minutes after the attack started.

During the remainder of the attack, Damage Control and Engineering personnel were busy isolating the damage and preparing the ship for sea. Since all of our work was below decks, we didn't witness any of the battle. However, we would hear tid-bits of information about the battle from time to time over a battle telephone system located at each battle station.

Occasionally, we would hear reports of a Japanese plane going down in flames. I don't recall the *Helena* receiving credit for any of the downed planes. Some of our gunners were sure they shot down one, possibly two. As was true throughout the war, ships claimed credit for two or three times the number of planes actually destroyed. With several ships firing at the same target, there was no way of knowing who should receive credit for the kill. This was the reason several ships would claim credit for the same downed plane.

The first phase of the attack lasted 30 minutes from 7:55 to 8:25AM. Over 90 percent of the damage the Japanese planes inflicted upon our ships, planes, and military installations during the attack, was accomplished during this 30-minute period.

The second phase, consisting of 170 planes struck at 8:40AM. The planes assigned to Pearl Harbor concentrated their attack on the Battleship *Nevada* (the same ship my dad was on during WWI) as she was heading for the open sea. But, now we were ready! Every anti-aircraft gun in the harbor opened fire. Consequently, very little damage was done. However, the *Nevada* was hit several times and forced aground near the harbor entrance.

Although severely damaged the *Helena* needed to be at sea. We were too tempting a target tied up to the dock.

The *Helena* was powered by four, steam-driven propellers. Two were put out of commission by the torpedo. Fortunately the other two, located just aft of the flooded compartments, were undamaged. Even so, a number of problems had to be overcome before they could be used.

First and foremost, they needed steam. Within minutes, the boilers in the Aft Fire Room were fired, but water was seeping in from the flooded compartments. Now there was a race between the rising water and the Boiler Room crew working to raise the steam pressure enough to power pumps to remove the water. The crew won with only minutes to spare.

Around 9:30 we were ready to get underway, but there were other problems. The minelayer, *Oglala*, was jammed against the *Helena*. Even with tugs it would take several hours to pull the *Oglala* clear of the *Helena*. Then there was the additional time needed to shore-up the bulkheads on both sides of the flooded compartments. If these bulkheads ruptured at sea, we would be, at best, unable to navigate, or worse, sink.

With all these problems, the chaotic situation plus witnessing what had happened to the *Nevada*, a decision was made to continue preparing to get underway, but to remain at dock-side until the situation stabilized or ordered to do otherwise.

By 9:45, all but 29 of the attacking Japanese planes had returned safely to their carriers. In less than 2 hours, over half of the aircraft we had positioned in and around Pearl Harbor had been destroyed. The Army and Navy had 481 planes on the islands when the attack started. The Japanese completely destroyed 271 and damaged over half of the remaining planes. Almost every ship in the harbor had been damaged, including 7 battleships sunk or heavily damaged. The Navy lost over 2,000 men killed with almost 1,000...including 17 sets of brothers-entombed aboard the battleship *Arizona*. The Army and Marines lost 307 men killed. There were 70 civilians killed. The *Helena* lost 29 men killed with 79 wounded.

During the attack, I was busy alongside other electricians cutting, splicing, and rerouting electrical circuits damaged by the torpedo. Between the first and second phase of the attack, the Officer-in-Charge of the Damage Control Unit, where I was stationed, asked for volunteers to remove several dead bodies located just outside the Forward Engine Room. I didn't volunteer. I had been by this area a few minutes before checking an electrical circuit nearby. It wasn't a pretty sight.

I have never forgotten the wide-eyed, terrified look on the face of one of these men. He was on his hands and knees seemingly still trying to escape but welded into that position by the fiery blast of the torpedo.

Words cannot describe the tension, fear, and anxiety we experienced during the remainder of the day. We had suffered devastating losses and expected more to come.

No one knew the location of the attacking Japanese Fleet!! But, we were convinced they would return for the kill. There were all kinds of rumors: from sabotage to troop landings. All proved to be false. The *Helena* could get underway, but certainly in no condition to seek out the enemy. I felt trapped. The thoughts of becoming a prisoner-of-war were real.

The night was even worse than the day. Everyone was mentally on edge. No one on the island slept that night. Our gunners were nervous and restless. Around 9PM, I witnessed four of our own planes, from the carrier *Enterprise*, with their landing lights on, being shot down by our own gunners as they attempted to land on Ford Island. They had given advance notice of their arrival, but somehow the word didn't reach one of our gunners on the beach. When he opened fire, every gun in the Harbor joined in. It was like a Fourth of July fireworks display!

As the sun rose on the morning of December 8, the tension began to subside. Fires were still burning out of control. The harbor was a mess with sunken and damaged ships, oil and debris was everywhere. But confidence began to replace the fear and anxiety of the day and night before.

Military strategists generally agree, the Japanese Pearl Harbor attack was skillfully planned and executed. However, the key factor in their victory was surprise. Had there been any warning, five, ten minutes, or more, the results would have been entirely different.

Of course, it could have been worse. None of our carriers were damaged. Usually one or more flat-top's were in harbor on weekends. They most assuredly would have been sunk. I shudder to think of the consequences had the Japanese followed up their attack with troop landings.

Did the Japanese use treachery and deceit to keep their Pearl Harbor plans a secret? The answer must be yes. Their ambassador was negotiating with our Secretary of State, in Washington, almost to the moment of the attack; with full knowledge their fleet was enroute to strike Pearl Harbor. This is treachery and deceit of the highest order.

However, the most controversial topic surrounding the Pearl Harbor attack and remains a controversy to this day: Did President Franklin Roosevelt know of the impending attack and deliberately withhold this information from our commanders in Hawaii?

I've been all over the board on this question. During the early years after the war, I was convinced that he knew and did, in fact, withhold this information from Admiral Kimmel

& General Short, our commanders in Hawaii. The reason: He wanted the United States in the war on the side of England to help defeat Germany. But, he knew the only way he could arouse the American people to support our entry into the war was for Japan to strike first. Therefore, he remained silent.

However, in recent years, after reading numerous articles, several books, and a Congressional Investigating Committee report, I have come to a different conclusion. True, there were signals that should have alerted our intelligence community, Cabinet Officers, and President Roosevelt to the impending attack. But, these signals were ignored! They were ignored simply because no one thought the Japanese had the audacity or resources to launch such a massive attack from their homeland some 3,000 miles away.

Although there were many acts of heroism during the attack, only a few medals were awarded, and none to the crew that had been aboard the *Helena*. Had we repulsed the attack, many more would have been cited for bravery. When things go wrong, we look for scapegoats not heroes. The scapegoats of the Pearl Harbor disaster were Admiral Kimmel and General Short, our Commanders in Hawaii. True, they deserve criticism for not having us more alert and better prepared for the attack.

But, higher ups in Washington-Secretary of the Army, Secretary of the Navy, Secretary of State Cordell Hull, and President Roosevelt share of the blame are inescapable. They had access to more intelligence information. They knew or should have known, negotiations with the Japanese had reached a crisis. They had information about Japan's plans to strike somewhere in the Pacific. It was their responsibility to alert Admiral Kimmel and General Short of the possibility of an attack.

It is clear they should have contacted our commanders by phone or special messenger and telling them: "Negotiations with Japan have reached a critical stage. We have information indicating they have plans to strike somewhere in the Pacific.

We don't believe it will be Hawaii, but we want you to be on maximum alert for the next 10 days". Had this been done, I'm confident we would have been ready for the attack.

Although only a few medals were awarded, clearly the crews of the various ships and stations fought in the best traditions of our military services. I know these traditions were held high aboard the *Helena*. Few would believe a confused, almost panic stricken group of men could turn themselves around in minutes and become an effective, efficient, and disciplined fighting force. But, it happened-not only aboard the *Helena*, but again and again on other ships and stations in and around Pearl Harbor that fateful day.

The Pearl Harbor attack signaled our entry into World War II. The world was at war. Our nation and the world would never be the same.

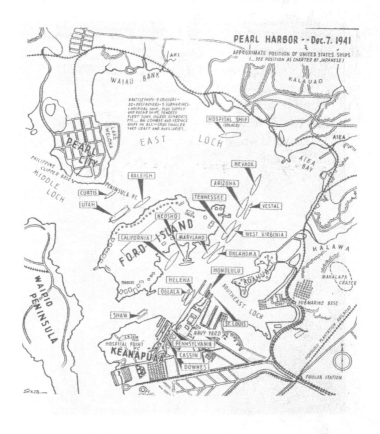

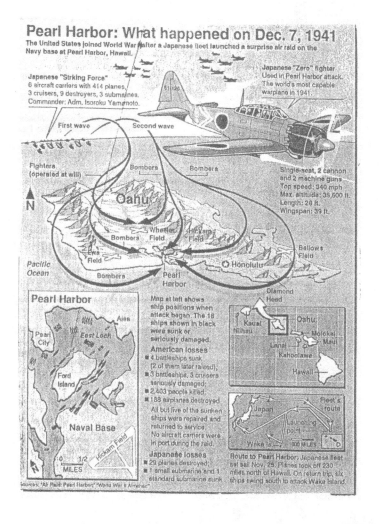

Pearl Harbor: What happened on Dec. 7, 1941

The United States joined World War II after a Japanese fleet launched a surprise air raid on the Navy base at Pearl Harbor, Hawaii.

Japanese "Striking Force"
6 aircraft carriers with 414 planes, 3 cruisers, 9 destroyers, 3 submarines. Commander: Adm. Isoroku Yamamoto.

Japanese "Zero" fighter Used in Pearl Harbor attack. The world's most capable warplane in 1941.

First wave
Second wave

Fighters (operated at will)
Bombers
Bombers

Single-seat, 2 cannon and 2 machine guns
Top speed: 340 mph
Max. altitude: 35,500 ft.
Length: 29 ft.
Wingspan: 39 ft.

N

Oahu

Wheeler Field
Hickam Field
Bombers
Ewa Field

Bellows Field

Pacific Ocean

Bombers
Pearl Harbor
Honolulu

Diamond Head

Pearl Harbor

Aiea
Pearl City
East Loch
Ford Island
Naval Base
Hickam Field

0   1/2
MILES

Sources: "Air Raid: Pearl Harbor," "World War II Almanac."

Map at left shows ship positions when attack began. The 18 ships shown in black were sunk or seriously damaged.

American losses
- 4 battleships sunk (2 of them later raised);
- 3 battleships, 3 cruisers seriously damaged;
- 2,403 people killed;
- 188 airplanes destroyed

All but five of the sunken ships were repaired and returned to service. No aircraft carriers were in port during the raid.

Japanese losses
- 29 planes destroyed;
- 1 small submarine and 1 standard submarine sunk

Kauai
Niihau
Oahu
Molokai
Lanai
Maui
Kahoolawe
Hawaii

Fleet's route
Japan
Launching point
Wake Is.
1000 MILES

Route to Pearl Harbor: Japanese fleet set sail Nov. 25. Planes took off 230 miles north of Hawaii. On return trip, six ships swing south to attack Wake Island.

OTHER NEWS IN 1941 –

Savings bonds and saving stamps were introduced. Folks across this nation began putting together "Bundles for Britain." Shipped more than 1 million tons of food to England.

OTHER NEWS IN 1942 –

American forces surrender to the Japanese at Bataan and Corregidor in the Pacific. Germany continued to bomb England.

Rationing stamps were introduced for food, clothing, and gasoline.

An industrialist, Henry Kaiser, developed a technique to build a ship in 4 days…The Liberty Ship.

One of my greatest fears going into battle during WWII was being trapped in a compartment below deck unable to get out if the ship sank. When the *Helena* was torpedoed and sank July 6, 1943, I'm sure many men were trapped in compartments with no possibility of escape because they were surrounded by water 120 feet below the surface of the water.

This happened to three men aboard the battleship West Virginia at Pearl Harbor. They lived for 16 days before oxygen was exhausted… There was a calendar on the wall a red "X " scratched through each of the dates from December 7 through December 23. I cannot imagine the horror they experienced.

Dec 31-41

NOTHING is to be written on this side except
to fill in the data specified. Sentences not required should be crossed out. IF ANYTHING ELSE IS
ADDED THE POSTCARD WILL BE DESTROYED.

I am well ~~(sick)~~

~~I have been admitted to hospital as~~ ~~(wounded)~~ ~~(not~~

~~Am getting on well. Hope to return~~
~~to duty soon.~~

~~I have received your~~ ~~(Letter dated~~
~~(Telegram dated~~
~~(Parcel dated~~

Letter follows at first opportunity.
~~I have received no letter from you~~ ~~(for a long time,~~
~~(lately.~~

Signature W. T. Davis
Date Dec. 9, 1941

We were not allowed to write home after the attack.
Instead every man on the HELENA was given a post
card like the one I received above. You will note
we were only allowed to sign our name, date, and
cross out the sentences that didn't apply.

My card was mailed December 9, 1941.. it arrived
home 3 weeks later..December 31..

Our mail was censored throughout the war, but this
card represents the most rigid we had to deal with.

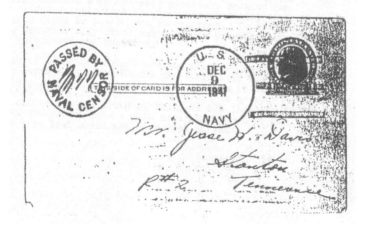

U.S.S. HELENA

December 11, 1941.
<u>To the Officers and Crew *of the U.S.S. HELENA.*</u>

I want to take advantage of a little lull after the treacherous attack of Sunday morning to express my gratitude to all my shipmates for the magnificent manner in which each of y o u, to the last man, upheld the traditions of the Navy on that historical occasion.

The Japanese, while hiding behind a peace mission in Washington, cowardly sneaked the first blow by striking us with bomb and torpedo before the battle was on. But this was their last blow at the *Helena*. Our guns were in action so quickly and so furiously they didn't any longer have the guts to face the music. Many subsequent attacks occurred over a three hour period, but, when confronted with the concentrated barrage of the *Helena*, the pilots were observed to turn away or fly so high their bombing was inaccurate. This prompt and decisive action on your part prevented the destruction of your own ship, and also assisted to the maximum degree in the preservation of other ships and objectives.

Every man did the right job at the right time. The machinery clicked throughout the engagement, and subsequent analyses fail to reveal a single mistake made. Every man stood unflinchingly by his station. Our engineers kept us in power for our guns; our damage control kept our ship machinery intact; our lookouts and bridge details kept the Japanese planes spotted; and, our gunners stood by their guns as veterans. In spite of early serious material casualties and the loss of many shipmates, our fire was continuous and decisive.

Instances of personal courage are too great to enumerate here. Let it suffice that the *Helena* has definitely won her place in history as a fighting ship which can give it always, and take it too when this must be done. I am proud to be your Captain and shipmate and we are all proud of the good old fighting *Helena*. Let us look to the future with a grim determination that our shipmates who were lost shall not have died in vain.

    R. H. ENGLISH
Captain, U.S. Navy,
Commanding

VALLEJO, CALIFORNIA JANUARY-JULY 1942

In war-time, the people at home have great compassion for the hardship and danger experienced by military personnel in combat situations. There is also sympathy for the families of these men and rightfully so. The mental strain they suffer is just as real as any borne by men on the battlefield. The agonizing torment our mother, father, and sisters endured from the moment the news of the Japanese attack hit the airways, until they heard from Roy & I, must have been devastating. After Pearl Harbor, over two thousand mothers and fathers never heard from their sons. There was only a telegram from the War Department telling them their son had been killed.

At Pearl Harbor, the days following the attack were hectic. Crews worked around the clock burying the dead, caring for the wounded, repairing the damage, and beefing up our defenses should the Japs return.

Within a week the *Helena* was placed in Dry Dock. After the water was drained from the flooded compartments, a special detail removed the bodies of the men trapped in the Forward Engine Room where the torpedo exploded. The remains of these men were removed in garbage cans.

The damage to the *Helena* was surveyed and considered too extensive for repairs to be made at Pearl Harbor. We were ordered back to the States for repairs. We were one happy crew!! Our thoughts turned from the war to the folks at home.

Temporary repairs were ordered. A steel plate was welded over the area damaged by the torpedo. The *Helena* was ready for the trip home.

In late December we were at sea on our way to the West Coast. Everyone breathed a sigh of relief as the *Helena* passed under the Golden Gate Bridge enroute to the Mare Island

Navy Yard located at Vallejo, California, about 30 miles north of San Francisco.

The Vallejo Yard was small compared to most other shipyards. They could handle no more than four or five ships at a time. In addition to their repair capabilities, they had spaces ("slips"-navy term), to build three ships from the keel up. Two submarines and a Tender were under construction when we arrived.

Ashore we soon discovered that the average citizen's attitude toward men in uniform had completely changed. Men in uniform were no longer shunned or ignored. Instead, people would go out of their way to speak to us. A few would even shake our hand and say they appreciated the job we were doing. Some even had tears in their eyes as they spoke. We were treated more like heroes than ordinary sailors everywhere we went.

During the early months of 1942, our forces in the Pacific suffered one defeat after another. Guam and the Philippines were lost. On the home front: Americans began to feel the effects of rationing. Ration stamps became more important than dollars. Rents, wages, and prices were frozen.

The war dominated the lives of every American. News broadcasts were the most popular programs on radio (no TV then). Every newspaper in the country used banner headlines to announce the latest news from the battle fronts. Movie cameramen covered every detail of the war around the world. War news was featured in every theatre across the nation. Movies began to have a war theme. Every new song reflected the mood of the times.

One of the popular songs at the time was, "I Don't Want to Set the World on Fire" followed by these words, "I just want to start a flame in your heart". A huge sign over the entrance to the Mare Island Navy Yard paraphrased this song in these words: "WE DON'T WANT TO SET THE WORLD

ON FIRE-WE JUST WANT TO START A FLAME IN TOKYO".

The unprovoked attack on Pearl Harbor generated bitter hatred among the American people toward the Japanese. On the West Coast some 80,000 Americans of Japanese descent and 40,000 illegal Japanese aliens were interned for the duration of the war because of the strong anti-Japanese sentiment and the risk of sabotage.

An update: In August, 1988 Congress passed, and President Reagan signed into law, a bill calling for the payment of $20,000 to each surviving American of Japanese descent, interned during World War II.

In June (before the bill passed) I wrote both Tennessee Senators and Congressman Jones, expressing my opposition to the bill's passage. Senator Gore and Sasser voted for the bill. Congressman Jones voted against its passage.

Senator Gore (former Vice-President Gore) said in a letter to me, to justify his vote, "80% of those interned were native born Americans". True, but he didn't tell the whole story. Nearly all of the parents and old folks were aliens. The children were American citizens simply because they were born here. Their parents made the decision to take them to relocation centers. To separate the families would have made a bad situation worse.

Many of those wounded at Pearl Harbor were being treated in hospitals in the Bay area. My best friend, Jim Wayland, was a patient at the hospital on the Naval Base. I visited him several times before the Navy transferred him to a hospital near his home in Dallas, Texas.

Jim and other patients on his ward were Navy Personnel wounded at Pearl Harbor. Most had flash burns on their face, arm, and legs. It was a ghastly sight. The medication used in treating their burns had formed a hard shell-like veneer over the burned areas. Only a few were recognizable at first glance.

I was visiting Jim, on one occasion, when a couple from the mid-west came in to see their son only a few beds away. He had first and second degree burns over most of his body and had lost almost half of his original weight. I watched as the couple paused at their son's bed, then moved on.

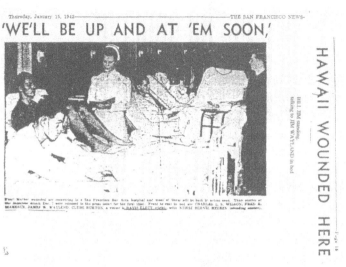

While still within hearing distance, they asked the orderly where their sons' bed was located. The orderly pointed to the bed they only seconds before had passed. It was a tearful reunion. There wasn't a dry eye on the ward. The young man died a week later.

With the ship undergoing repairs, there was little for the crew to do except monitor the work of the Navy Yard workers. It was a time of maximum leave and liberty.

In March, Roy and I went home on leave for two weeks. Our family, friends, and neighbors couldn't have been nicer. We were treated like celebrities. We were the featured guests at the weekly luncheon meeting of the Covington Lion's club. At the conclusion of the meeting one of the members took us to the Covington Grammar School for his son and daughter to see two "war heroes".

I never considered myself a hero. I had only done my duty at Pearl Harbor, like thousands of others. Nothing but a miracle kept me out of harm's way. We were given special recognition simply because we were among the first home from the war zone after the war started.

Back in Vallejo, our thoughts shifted from home to having fun. My liberty habits shifted from sightseeing to going ashore with shipmates visiting bars and night clubs in San Francisco. I had my first drink of alcohol in Honolulu on my 21st birthday. Now I began to drink more, possibly to excess on occasions, but I was careful not to go over the edge. I could never understand why so many of my shipmates would drink themselves into a drunken stupor, not knowing where they had been, what they had done, or how they got back to the *Helena*.

Over half of the single members of the crew spent their liberties in San Francisco, less than an hour away by bus. They would usually go to the same night spot every time they were in San Francisco…Not me…I would visit at least two, sometimes three or four an evening. I always thought there would be better music and a livelier crowd at the next stop.

The most unusual bar I remember was located on one of the main streets downtown, just a few blocks from the Oakland Ferry. It featured "The Girl in a Gold Fish Bowl". Above the bar was, what appeared to be, an oversized underwater bowl. During short intervals throughout the evening, a girl would appear almost nude swimming like a mermaid. I'm quite sure it was done with mirrors, with the girl in another room… probably not even wet.

Another favorite liberty town was Sacramento, the California State Capitol, about 60 miles north of Vallejo. There was bus service, but it was much easier to hitchhike to & from. Since we were in uniform, only a few cars would go by before a driver would stop and take us to our destination.

A short time after we arrived, a British Cruiser was placed in Dry Dock next to the *Helena*. The entire bow of the ship had been blown off by a German torpedo in the battle for the island of Crete, off the coast of Greece. Instead of moving forward, the ship had made the entire trip from the Mediterranean Sea to Vallejo stern first. The remains of some forty British sailors were removed from the flooded compartments within hours after the ship was placed in Dry Dock.

The British were friendly, but we never socialized much at the Navy Yard or ashore. Shortly after we arrived, the entire *Helena* crew was invited to a social hour aboard the British ship. The only part of the program I remember was the song "Maria Elena", sung by a British sailor. To this day, it is my all-time favorite song.

After three months in Vallejo, I began to feel a sense of urgency about my life. My thoughts kept going back to my dead and wounded shipmates, the destruction, treachery and deceit of the Japanese in attacking Pearl Harbor. I knew we would soon be returning to the war zone. I could be wounded or killed. If I somehow made it safely, it would be months, possibly a year or more before we would be returning to the States. I knew I had to cram a lot of living into a few weeks. It was eat, drink, and be merry time!

During the early part of 1942, none of the news from the Pacific was good. The Japanese were in control of the Pacific, west of Hawaii and north of Australia.

In April, we began to fight back. The carrier *Hornet*, using US Army Air Force medium bombers, launched an attack on Tokyo, some 600 miles from the Japanese mainland. Instead of returning to the *Hornet* after the raid, they landed on the mainland of China. The raid had very little military value, but it gave the spirits of the American people a much needed lift, after weeks of nothing but depressing news.

In May, the Battle of Carol Sea (in the South Pacific) slowed the Japanese advance toward Australia. In June, during the Battle of Midway (in the Central Pacific) Japan lost 4 carriers. We lost one carrier. This battle proved the turning point in the war with Japan in our favor.

Repairs to the *Helena* were completed in late June. The damage to the hull, machinery, and equipment were restored to like-new condition. In addition, the latest in radar equipment was installed. The troublesome 1.1 anti-aircraft guns were replaced with more effective and potent 40MM guns. The *Helena* was now as modern as any ship in the Navy. We were ready for action.

Although I was enjoying every minute of our stay, I was glad to see it come to an end. I wanted to be where the action was. Today, I find this feeling difficult to believe or explain.

For one thing, there was a personal score to settle with the Japanese. For another, there was a feeling of being left out of the war. I was safe and secure in the States. Looking back, it seems stupid to want to risk my life in battle. Call it patriotism or a sense of duty; I only know I would have been miserable had I been reassigned to shore duty or a non-combat ship.

In early July, the *Helena* left San Francisco for the South Pacific, where the Japanese were massing their forces to take over the New Hebrides Islands. The *Helena* would play an important role in preventing this from happening.

GUADALCANAL JULY-NOVEMBER 1942

The tension and stress of war began to build as the *Helena* cleared the California Coast. The latest news indicated the Japanese had started to move south from New Guinea to the Solomon Islands. Their purpose was to cut our lines of communication between Hawaii and Australia.

Captain Read's announcement, a few hours at sea, only confirmed our convictions-we would rendezvous with our forces in the Pacific during the first two weeks of August.

In port or at sea, every member of the crew has day-to-day duties and responsibilities which keep them busy from 8AM to 5PM. It could be simply a cleaning assignment (several times a day you could hear the command, "Now hear this, clean sweep down fore and aft") or it could be replacing light bulbs, or maintenance and upkeep of radar, gunnery, or telephone equipment-just to name a few.

In port much of the ship's machinery is shut down entirely or operated on a very limited basis. Although the *Helena* had evaporators to convert salt water into fresh water and generators for electricity, we always obtained these services from shore whenever they were available. At sea, the *Helena* operated entirely on its own. The ship's propulsion machinery, boilers, and other related equipment had to be manned around the clock. The ship must maintain a proper course, communications must be maintained with other units, and visual as well as electronic surveillance must be maintained at all times. In a War Zone, we had 150 to 200 men on duty at all times.

Because of the additional requirements at sea, almost every man in the Engineering Department(to a varying degree in other departments) were required to stand watch-usually four hours on duty with eight hours off. Of course, in a War Zone, the Gunnery Department had personnel stationed at various gun stations for quick response to enemy attack.

Because of the damage suffered by our ships at Pearl Harbor, the Navy began to place great emphasis on Damage Control. Should a ship be damaged in battle, it is of utmost importance that repairs be made as quickly as possible. Everything must be done to keep the ship in fighting-trim at all times.

At the Mare Island Navy Yard I was placed in charge of the Electrical section of the *Helena's* Damage Control System. It was my responsibility to know the electrical system of the *Helena* from stem to stern. For example, in the event electricity was knocked out to a particular gun mount, I was supposed to not only know the nearest alternate source of power, but to supervise a temporary hook-up.

I spent hours tracing circuits on blue prints. I would physically follow each circuit from its source through watertight bulkheads (walls) from compartment to compartment until the cable reached its destination at a motor or switch box.

I made drawings of the maze of cables as they passed through the various bulkheads. A copy of these drawings was at each of three Repair Stations. I wanted my men to be able to identify the right cable anywhere on the ship should it become necessary to cut a particular cable. To cut the wrong cable would make a bad situation even worse.

It was my custom to go topside several times a day at sea for fresh air and just to watch the *Helena* glide through the water. The *Helena* was an impressive looking fighting machine. I was confident it was the best ship in the Navy.

The *Helena* was equipped with two single float biplanes (Curtis Socs), which were always in place ready to be launched from two Catapults located on the stern of the *Helena*. Launching and retrieving these planes was an interesting operation to observe.

To launch the planes, a 60-foot Catapult platform would be trained over the side of the ship. The pilot would throttle the engine to maximum RPM's. The Catapult Officer would then signal to launch the plane. At that instant a powder charge would be fired in a cylinder that would hurl the plane from one end of the Catapult to the other, at speeds up to 60 or 70 miles per hour, the take-off speed of the plane.

On August 7, we were near the International Date Line when word was received that our Marines had landed on Guadalcanal, an island in the Solomon group of islands. This was the first offensive action by our forces in the Pacific and we were elated.

Two days later, we received some bad news. In a night action near Savo Island (near Guadalcanal) on August 8-9, the Japanese had completely crushed our forces. Our losses, three US Cruisers sunk, One US Cruiser severely damaged, and one Australian Cruiser sunk. The Japanese suffered only superficial losses. It was the worst defeat ever suffered by the US Navy at sea.

On August 11, we anchored in the Harbor at Port Villa, the capital of the New Hebrides Islands. These islands are several hundred miles south of the Solomons, where the Battle for Guadalcanal was taking place.

The Port Villa Harbor is an ideal sanctuary for ships. There are mountains on all sides with only a narrow channel to the sea. The water was a light shade of blue. Add to this the lush green vegetation which extended from the water's edge to the mountain tops and you had a picture book setting.

During our stay, which lasted four days, I was ashore only once. Two observations come to mind. The natives were black with sandy reddish Afro-styled hair. They used long hand-hued boats for fishing which made me think of scenes from the movie "Mutiny on the Bounty".

In contrast to the beauty of the scenery from a distance, was the filth around the village near the shoreline. I can still remember the huge rusty-colored, cat-size rats which romped from hole to hole that honeycombed the dock area. They acted more like pets than vermin. I felt dirty during my 30-odd minutes ashore.

We were in the War Zone but away from the fighting arena. It is a strange feeling to be in an area where things are happening, itching for a fight, yet not be a part of the action.

During the third week in August, we were assigned to the Carrier *Wasp* Task Force. Now we would surely see some action for the war was becoming more of an air war with each passing day. Just being part of such a force was a thrilling experience. Nothing is more majestic than a carrier at sea with planes circling overhead.

There were three Carrier Task Forces operating in the area at the time. Each group acted independently of the other with their own screening forces, made up of Cruisers and Destroyers. In our group there were four Cruisers and six Destroyers spread over a two or three mile radius around the *Wasp*.

The Battle of the Eastern Solomons was fought on August 24. The Japanese committed three Carriers, three Battleships, nine Cruisers, thirteen Destroyers, and 36 submarines to this engagement. We had three Carrier Groups (*Enterprise, Saratoga,* and *Wasp*) in position for the battle on August 23.

However, Admiral Fletcher, commander of our Carrier Forces, had information placing the Japanese forces some 600 miles away near Truk, their big Naval Base in the Central Pacific. Believing there would be no battle for several days, he ordered the *Wasp* group south for refueling on the afternoon of the 23rd.

The two opposing forces discovered each other the next morning about 250 miles apart. At the time, we were about 100 miles further south and missed the action. The battle was considered a stand-off. The Japanese lost one small carrier. The *Enterprise* received three bomb hits, killing 75 men and was out of action for several months.

Meanwhile, our Marines and the Japanese on Guadalcanal were engaged in a death struggle for control of the island. During the day American ships would land reinforcements and supplies for our forces. At night the Japanese, using fast Destroyers (we called them the "TOKYO EXPRESS"), would land troops and supplies for their troops.

It is difficult to understand the situation around Guadalcanal during those dark days. Our ships and planes had control of the area during the daylight hours, but at night the Japanese took over.

On September 14, the Carrier *Wasp* and *Hornet* task groups were assigned to provide protection for six Transports carrying Marine replacements to Guadalcanal. On September 15, two Japanese submarines penetrated our Destroyer screen. The *Wasp* was hit by 3 torpedoes and sank. One torpedo hit the Battleship *North Carolina*, taking her out of action for several months. Another torpedo hit & sank the Destroyer *O'Brien*.

At the time of the attack, I was in the aft Boiler Room checking electrical cables as they passed from the Boiler Room into the aft Engine Room. I was behind one of the steam boilers and did not know of the attack until I noticed we were slowing down, then speed up, then changing course in one direction then another.

By setting a zigzag course, our Captain was making the *Helena* a difficult target for the submarine to hit. No torpedoes were fired in our direction. I shudder to think of my fate had the *Helena* been hit. I was below the water line, the most hazardous location during a torpedo attack.

We picked up about 1,000 survivors from the *Wasp*. We unloaded them at Espiritu Santos, where they were assigned other ships in the area. During this critical period, survivors were assigned to other ships again and again. (Later, when the *Helena* sank, we had men aboard who had survived the sinking of two and three ships previously)

During the remainder of our stay in the South Pacific, the *Helena* and other Cruisers, Destroyers, and Supply Ships used the harbor at Espiritu Santos as our main base of operations. The harbor at Neomea, in New Caledonia, was the main base for Carriers, Battleships, and Transports.

On September 25, Captain Read (who had assumed command six months earlier at Vallejo) turned over command of the *Helena* to Captain C.C. Hoover. I don't recall any explanation given for the change. We were hoping for the best Captain in the Navy, for the life of every man on board in battle or any emergency is dependent upon the skill of one man, the Captain.

As an enlisted man, you never get to know the Captain personally unless your duty or battle station happens to be on the Bridge. Otherwise, you learn of their ability to command from scuttlebutt (rumors) and the day-to-day orders handed down through the chain-of-command.

Captain Read never generated confidence among the crew in his ability as a leader. Although, in fairness to him, he was never fully tested in battle. One example of what I am talking about...we were required to wear white uniforms topside unless our work assignment required dungarees. The crew felt like a fool wearing full-dress uniforms while the *Wasp* survivors were coming on board. A small item to be sure, but we had the impression that Captain Read could not shake peace-time Navy routine for war-time realities. We were in a War Zone. It was a time for relaxed rules and regulations.

Shortly after the WASP was sunk, the *Helena* with three other Cruisers and five Destroyers were organized into a new Task Group labeled 64.2. Our purpose was to run interference for Transports and Supply units furnishing men and supplies to our forces on Guadalcanal. We had another even more important mission... to stop the "TOKYO EXPRESS". The Commander of Task Force 64.2 was Rear Admiral Scott with headquarters on the Cruiser *San Francisco*.

The first test of the new type of "Screen and Attack" force came on the night of October 11-12, in the Battle of Cape Esperance, less than three weeks following the date Task Group 64.2 was formed. Hardly time for the Admiral to know the strength and weakness of the ships under his command.

There was certainly not enough time to develop the skill and confidence the Japanese had mastered in night action in and around Guadalcanal since the Marines landed on August 7. Each time we had dared to stand up to the Japanese at night, we had been soundly defeated.

However, our forces had one important edge, not yet placed into service by the Japanese...Radar. A device that could detect ships at great distances and pin-point their location, day or night, thereby providing the data our gunners needed to fire accurately. But, Radar was in its early development stage. Few commanders, including Admiral Scott, understood the capabilities and advantages Radar gave our ships in night action. Although the *Helena* and *Boise* had the very latest in Radar equipment, Admiral Scott had selected the *San Francisco* as his Flagship. A decision which almost spelled disaster in the upcoming engagement.

On October 9 and 10, we were patrolling South and East of Guadalcanal providing a screen for Transports scheduled to arrive on October 13. Each day around noon, we would change course and head north. We would continue on this course until in the vicinity of Cape Esperance, near the Northeast coast of Guadalcanal. When no enemy contacts were reported, we would turn around and return to our daytime screening position.

On the afternoon of the 11th, near sunset, Admiral Scott signaled, "We're going in. Jap force, believed to be two Cruisers and six Destroyers."

What we didn't know at the time, not even Admiral Scott knew (I didn't have this information until I read accounts taken from official Japanese and American records in 1977) the Japanese had sent two groups of ships south that night. The first group, made up of two Seaplane Tenders and six Destroyers, were loaded with troops and supplies. The second group, consisting of three Cruisers and two Destroyers, was in support of the first group and had orders to shell Henderson Airfield on Guadalcanal.

The first group was in the vicinity of Guadalcanal at 9:45PM. Soon thereafter, they were anchored and unloading troops and supplies. Movements of both groups were co-ordinated by Japanese Naval Headquarters so that the second group would arrive in the target about two hours after the arrival of the first group. The two hour period, plus the time taken by the Support Group to shell the airfield, would give the reinforcement group ample time to complete unloading operations. Then the two groups would join forces and head home. By 11:45pm, the second group was near its objective.

At 10:30PM, Scott ordered our Task Group to form into a single file formation, with three Destroyers in the lead, followed by the *San Francisco, Boise, Salt Lake City, Helena* and two Destroyers bringing up the rear. The column, about three miles in length, was placed on an easterly course pointed in the direction of Savo Island and parallel to the Northern coast of Guadalcanal.

At 11:33, with the Task Force near and almost on a collision course with Savo Island, Scott ordered the column to execute a U-turn, which would place the formation on a westerly course, virtually in the same relative position as before. He wanted to maintain a position between Savo Island and Cape Esperance, the area the Japanese normally traveled on their runs to Guadalcanal. However...

There was a foul-up in the column movement. The three lead Destroyers made the proper turn, but the Captain of the *San Francisco* (the Flagship), misinterpreted the Admiral's signal. Instead of following in the wake of the three Destroyers ahead, he cut sharply to the left leaving the three Destroyers astern of the column. The other ships followed the Flagship.

The counter-march was completed at 11:42. The *San Francisco* was now at the head of the formation. The three Destroyers previously in the lead were now on the starboard side and astern of the column.

My battle station, a Damage Control Unit located on the second deck amidships, had not changed since Pearl Harbor. In battle, Damage Control personnel have little to do except wait. Whether or not we performed any function depended entirely upon whether or not the *Helena* was damaged by gun fire, bomb, or torpedo. Even though there were 12 to 15 men in our unit, few words were spoken in the three hours since General Quarters had sounded. Our attention was riveted on the man wearing the phone head set. He would relay information he picked up from the Bridge, Radar, and other stations on the circuits scattered throughout the ship.

At 11:30, Radar reported an enemy contact about 14 miles away. At 11:33, Radar reported three contacts 12 miles away. This was about the time Scott ordered the column to reverse course. We thought we were maneuvering into a better position to open fire.

At 11:38, we completed our turn. Radar reported five contacts at nine miles. What were we waiting for? The contacts were within range of even our five inch guns.

At 11:42, Captain Hoover reported to Admiral Scott that the contacts were at six miles. The Flagship acknowledged his report with a "Roger", but no other response.

At 11:45, Captain Hoover asked permission for the *Helena* to open fire. Another "Roger" to acknowledge receipt of the message. Apparently the Admiral thought the contacts were our own ships. But, Hoover was certain they were not the three destroyers in the mixed-up column movement.

Hoover waited a few seconds. He again requested permission to open fire. When the second acknowledgement was "Roger", he ordered our guns to "Commence Firing". We learned later that Scott had not intended to authorize the *Helena* to open fire. He was still weighing the possibility that the reported targets were our own ships.

The waiting was terrible. The loneliness and helplessness made every nerve in my body stand on edge. It was a relief when *Helena's* fifteen 6-inch and four 5-inch guns opened fire. The ship shuddered and shook with each salvo. We continued firing without let-up until Radar reported the first target had disappeared from the radar scope. There was a pause in the firing.

A few seconds later, we were firing at a new target. We fired off and on until 12:20AM when Admiral Scott gave orders to break off the engagement and set a course south-west. We fired 340 rounds of five-inch ammunition and 560 rounds of six-inch ammunition during the engagement.

From the moment the battle started, the formation started to disintegrate. It was almost a case of every ship acting alone. This condition exists in all fighting in close quarters, whether it is hand-to-hand combat between armies on land or a dog-fight between planes in the air.

Had the battle been fought at a distance of ten to twelve miles, our Task Force would possibly have remained intact. In this instance (from Japanese official records), two ships of the Japanese Task Force, a Cruiser and Destroyer, slipped undetected past the stern of the column less than two minutes after the battle started. A short time later, they turned around and started firing at us.

American news reports said we sank four destroyers, a cruiser, and a transport. Admiral Scott thought we had sunk three Cruisers and four Destroyers. There is no way to avoid duplication in a battle like this one. Usually, every ship firing at the same target will claim credit for the kill.

In addition, there is always the tendency to maximize the enemy's losses while minimizing your own losses. This makes for good propaganda, an important factor in war. It is good for the morale at home as well as the men fighting on the front lines. Men on the front lines must always believe they are hurting the enemy more than the enemy is hurting them to be at their best.

Actually, from official Japanese records, only one Destroyer was sunk at the battle scene. Two Cruisers were damaged, one so severely damaged that it sank the next morning. The other Cruiser was hit many times causing a number of casualties, including the Task Force Commander Admiral Goto, but the *Aoba* returned safely to her base. The Cruiser and Destroyer that passed astern of our formation, returned to base without any damage.

Tokyo news accounts stated their forces had destroyed two of our Cruisers and one Destroyer. Actually, we lost one Destroyer (the *Duncan*) along with the lives of 87 members of her crew. The *Boise* was hit seven times, killing 37 and wounding many more. The damage forced her out of action for several months. The *Salt Lake City* was also heavily damaged, receiving two hits, and out of service for weeks.

The Destroyer *Farenholt* was hit twice by our own ships and out of action for several weeks. There is evidence to indicate that the *Duncan* was sunk by our own guns. Shooting down our own planes and sinking our own ships, although rare, happened again and again during the war.

Once a battle starts, especially at night, it is almost impossible to distinguish, with certainty, friend or foe. Sometimes a friendly ship will simply get in the line of fire at the enemy, which is what happened in the case of the *Farenholt*. In most situations, it is simply a question of not being sure. When a battle heats up, the decision to fire or not to fire at a target often has only one rationale, when in doubt fire! This may have happened in the sinking of the *Duncan*.

The *San Francisco, Helena*, and three of our Destroyers were not damaged during the engagement. At day break, the same morning, we were released from battle stations. We were exhausted, but a happy and proud crew. We had entered the enemy's own back yard and beat him decisively.

Reading accounts of the engagement today, with all the facts on both sides available, the battle can be viewed in an entirely different light. The big winner that night was luck! The counter-march foul up, causing Admiral Scott to delay firing, when the enemy was within firing range, almost spelled disaster for our entire Task Force.

Another important factor was a lack of alertness on the part of the Japanese. They should have spotted us long before we opened fire. In the Battle of Savo Island, they sighted our forces at a distance of seven miles. Had they opened fire first, the results would have been entirely different.

The most important decision made during the engagement was the one made by our skipper, Captain Hoover. He opened fire to start the battle. We won the battle because our skipper opened fire without direct order to do so by our Task Force Commander. Disobedience? Not in light of the outcome. Especially, when you consider the consequences had he not acted as he did. Needless to say, Captain Hoover was an instant hero to the *Helena* crew. I doubt if any ship's Captain during WWII was more respected, admired, or loved. This feeling would deepen in the days to follow.

After a few days in Espiritu Santos, loading ammunition and supplies, we were back at sea patrolling off the coast of the Solomon Islands. The heavy Cruiser *Chester* joined our task force, as a replacement for the *Salt Lake City* and *Boise*, who had been ordered back to the states for repairs. The *Chester* lasted less than a week. On the night of October 20, at 10:20PM, a Japanese Submarine, I-176, launched several torpedoes at our formation. One of the torpedoes struck the *Chester*, forcing her out of action for months. The average life of a ship, without being knocked out of action or worse, during this period was less than 30 days.

The later part of October and the first two weeks of November was a critical period in the Battle for Guadalcanal. The Japanese High Command was mounting an all out effort to take over Henderson Field. They were determined to push us off the Island, regardless of the cost. We were just as determined to hang on.

The Japanese were building up their forces at night. We were adding to our forces during the daylight hours. Their Navy units would shell our forces at night. Our Navy would blast their positions during the day. On the morning of November 4, at 9:20AM, the *Helena, San Francisco*, and Destroyer *Sterett*, shelled Japanese positions at Kolumbona Point on Guadalcanal. The *Helena* fired 1276 rounds of six-inch and 448 rounds of five-inch ammunition.

Although we did not know it at the time, the Battle for Guadalcanal was fast approaching a climax. The next two weeks would determine if the Japanese would force us off the island or not. The *Helena* was destined to play an important role in the outcome.

GUADALCANAL TO SYDNEY, NOVEMBER 1942 - APRIL 1943

Between the first and tenth of November, the Japanese unloaded 67 cruiser and destroyer loads of troops on Guadalcanal. By the 12th of November, the Japanese forces outnumbered our troops for the first time since the initial landing on August 7.

On November 11, our Task Force was again off the coast of Guadalcanal providing a screen for four transports unloading men and supplies. Another Task Force, headed by the light cruiser *Atlanta*, was assigned to protect three more transports engaged in the same operation.

Everything went smoothly and quietly on the 11th. By late afternoon, the *Atlanta* Transport Group had completed unloading operations and pulled away from the landing area.

At 7:18AM the next morning (November 12), the *Helena* along with four destroyers began shelling Japanese positions at Lunga Point. Before 8:30AM, the *Helena* had fired 494 rounds of six-inch ammunition and 201 rounds of five-inch ammunition.

By mid-morning, the transports in our group were near the halfway point in their unloading operations. About noon, Coast Watchers stationed some 100 miles north, reported approximately 30 Japanese planes heading south. Our transports were ordered away from the docking area. They were at sea before the planes arrived a few minutes after 1PM.

When the planes came into view they were flying at low altitudes, no more than a few hundred feet above the water. Every anti-aircraft gun in our Task Force opened fire. Black bursts of exploding shells filled the air in the vicinity of the incoming twin-engine planes.

The planes dropped to less than a 100 feet above the water to begin their torpedo run. Several were hit and spun into the water. The others launched their torpedoes. None hit their target.

Only one ship in our Task Force was damaged in the attack. A plane, hit by gunfire crashed into the aft superstructure of the *San Francisco*. There were a number of casualties, but the damage was slight permitting her to continue as our flagship. I learned in 1990 that a resident of Tipton County, Finnie "Red" Cates, was among those killed aboard the *San Francisco*. There is a memorial marker honoring him in the Drummonds cemetery.

Anti-aircraft guns shot down nine planes. Our fighter pilots, from Henderson Field, got most of the rest. Although the *Helena* claimed three at the time, there is no way of knowing how many we shot down, if any. We fired 193 rounds of five-inch and hundreds of rounds of 40MM and 20MM Anti-aircraft shells at the attacking planes.

The remains of several Jap planes could be seen floating around for some time after the attack. I remember one in particular. The pilot was standing on the fuselage of his half-submerged plane apparently not injured by the gunfire or crash.

He did not seem to move a muscle or bat an eye as the *Helena* passed no more than 100 yards away. You had to admire his courage. In spite of being shot down and in the midst of hundreds of enemy guns he could still stand tall.

The pilot was still in sight when I heard a 20MM gun, on another ship, open fire. The pilot was hit and knocked down. Even then, the gunner continued to fire, as other guns joined in, until his motionless body disappeared from view. I have often wondered if the results would have been the same had the pilot waved a white flag or raised his hands to surrender.

What can anyone say about such madness, other than war brings out the beast in man. Inhuman acts were committed by both sides. There were reports of Japanese pilots firing at our pilots as they tried to parachute to safety after their plane was disabled. There were instances of Japanese units waving a white flag, indicating they wanted to surrender. As soon as our Marines came into view to take prisoners, other Japs would open fire from concealed positions.

As night approached, we escorted our transports south for greater safety, as we had on the 11th. However, instead of staying with the transports we reversed our course and headed back to Savo Island.

Unknown to the enlisted members of the crew at the time, our Task Force Commanders had received information from search planes and Coastwatchers, the TOKYO EXPRESS was heading south toward Guadalcanal. The force was one of the largest ever assembled by the Japanese. It included two battleships, one cruiser and eleven destroyers.

Ordinarily, five cruisers and eight destroyers would not dare engage such a formidable force. However, this was not an ordinary situation. The Battle for Guadalcanal had reached a critical stage. We could not afford to let such a large bombardment group blast our positions on Guadalcanal.

On the night of October 13-14, when a smaller but similar force shelled our positions, 48 planes were destroyed, several hundred Marines were killed or wounded, and Henderson Field was out of commission for several days. Our Commanders had but one choice. American battleships were too far away to give any assistance. Somehow this out-gunned and out-numbered Task Force must prevent the Japanese from shelling our positions on Guadalcanal, even if every ship had to be sacrificed.

For the superstitious, even the number of ships and the date foretold the worst…13 American ships going into battle on Friday the 13th. Before the sun rose the next morning, eight American ships would be sunk, hundreds of sailors, and two Admirals would be killed.

61

Soon after darkness fell on the 12th, we were at our battle stations. Admiral Callaghan, who had replaced Admiral Scott on the *San Francisco*, (Scott was now second in command using the *Atlanta* as his Flagship) had the Task Force move into a single file formation. Four destroyers were in the lead, followed by the *Atlanta, San Francisco, Portland, Helena, Juneau*, with four more destroyers in the rear.

The hours slipped by without incident until 1:20AM, when radar reported three contacts in the vicinity of Savo Island. Minutes later the number of contacts increased. By 1:30AM radar was reporting 18 objects on their scope, including two exceptionally large units in the oncoming Japanese Task Force.

At this moment the Japanese were not aware of our presence. As the range between the two forces began to close, the suspense I had experienced during the October 11-12 battle began to build. Our column was on a course designed to intercept the Japanese units before they reached Guadalcanal. The range between the two forces began dropping, ten, seven, five miles. Why was it taking them so long to open fire??

Admiral Callaghan was making the same mistake Admiral Scott had in the October engagement. He had little or no confidence in radar. As a consequence, he failed to act on the information he was receiving from the *Helena* and other ships with radar, about the speed and range of the enemy force.

Captain Hoover did not ask permission to open fire as he had in the Battle of Cape Esperance because our column was not in a position to fire. Our ships were aimed like an arrow straight at the enemy force. For good firing position, we needed to be blocking their advance or parallel to the enemy force. Naval ships need to fire "broadsides", either port or starboard, in order to bring the maximum number of guns to bear on a target. Instead, we continued to head straight at the enemy formation.

At 1:40AM, the *Cushing*, our lead destroyer, was forced to alter course to avoid colliding with two Japanese destroyers, who were part of the screen for their battleships. This incident signaled the beginning of one of the wildest naval battles in history.

By his failure to act timely, Admiral Callaghan could no longer use surprise to his advantage. In addition, he began to lose control over the ships under his command. The four lead destroyers were scattered among the Japanese units after almost colliding with the oncoming fleet. Only the five Cruisers following four destroyers remained in column formation.

Admiral Abe, the Japanese Task Force Commander, not expecting a naval battle, had to change his plans. He immediately ordered his ships to change from bombardment to armor piercing type ammunition.

The near collision and the resulting disorder at the head of his column caused Admiral Callaghan to hesitate about opening fire for fear of hitting his own ships. The suspense was awful. Radar was reporting contacts all over the place. Yet we had not opened fire!!

Suddenly the Bridge reported a searchlight (aboard a Japanese destroyer less than a mile away) illuminating ships in our column. The time was 1:48AM, a full eight minutes after the near collision at the head of our column. I expected the *Helena* to immediately open fire. But seconds, which seemed like hours, passed before our guns began firing.

Almost at this instance, we heard a splattering sound on the deck above. The sound was like hail hitting a tin roof. The next morning, an inspection revealed that a small Japanese shell (three to five inch) had hit one of our smoke stacks.

Shrapnel from the exploding shell hit the metal deck above our head causing the sound we heard. The shrapnel also killed an electrician stationed on the searchlight platform only a few feet from the exploding shell.

With searchlights pinpointing the location of our column, the Japanese opened fire. The *Atlanta* was their initial target. Some of the first shells killed Admiral Scott and his staff. In seconds, the *Atlanta* was ablaze from stem to stern and had to drop out of the column.

With the *Atlanta* out of action, Admiral Callaghan directed the remainder of his ships between the two Jap battleships (the *Hiei* to the left and the *Kirishima* to the right). At one point, we were firing simultaneously at targets on our left and right.

Soon the scene looked like a gigantic Fourth of July fireworks display. Flares and star shells lighted a 10-mile wide area. Shells criss-crossed over, in front of and behind us. The *Helena* would fire a salvo or two then cease firing-pause 10-15 seconds then fire again-then repeat with short salvos with varying periods of silence. We would speed up, slow down, change course, first in one direction, then another. Sometimes such action was necessary to miss a torpedo heading our way. There were geysers in the water from near misses. Burning ships dotted the area. Within minutes, it was impossible to identify friend or foe unless at point-blank range.

I can appreciate the feeling of the six hundred who rode into the valley of death in Tennyson's "Charge of the Light Brigade". Only skillful ship handling and ingenious firing tactics by Captain Hoover, plus some luck, brought us through.

After shooting our way through the Jap force in one direction, we reversed course and waded through again when the Jap force counter-marched and headed home. In the melee, the destroyers *Laffey, Monssen, Barton*, and *Cushing* were sunk. The destroyers *O'Brien* and *Aaron Ward* were heavily damaged. The superstructure of the *San Francisco* was riddled with exploding shells, killing Admiral Callaghan and the ship's Captain. Almost every man on the main deck and above were either killed or wounded.

The *Atlanta* had to be scuttled before noon. The *Juneau* had been torpedoed, but still able to maintain headway. The *Portland* had been torpedoed in the stern and could only be steered in circles. The destroyer *O'Brien* was only slightly damaged. The *Helena* received only three small caliber shell hits... one on the main deck forward, the stack amidships, and on #4 six inch turret aft. Nothing serious with only one man killed and 20 wounded. By some miracle, the destroyer *Fletcher* was spared, the only ship in our Task Force without a scratch.

The Japanese lost two destroyers, with two heavily damaged. The Battleship *Kirishima*, a cruiser, and two destroyers were only slightly damaged. The Battleship *Hiei* was heavily damaged by shells and torpedoes. She was sunk by our planes in mid-morning, only five miles north of Savo Island. The *Hiei* was the first battleship sunk by American forces in the war. Six of their destroyers went through the battle unharmed.

The battle ended at 2:26AM. Our skipper, Captain Hoover, was now in charge of the Task Force, since he was the senior officer aboard the ships able to navigate under their own power. He ordered all ships to join the *Helena* as he set a course south away from the battle area. Of the 13 American ships entering the battle, only six were able to respond-the *Helena, San Francisco, Juneau*, and three destroyers. The *Helena* fired 695 rounds of five and six-inch ammunition in the battle.

I was exhausted both physically and mentally. Breakfast was served, but few could eat. My stomach was in a knot. I was too keyed up to relax or sleep.

About mid-morning, the *San Francisco* requested additional doctors and medical supplies to properly treat the more than 100 men severely wounded in the battle. At 11AM, approximately 20 miles west of San Christobal Island, we slowed almost to a stop to transfer medical personnel and supplies from the *Helena* and *Juneau* to the *San Francisco*.

I went topside to observe our motor whale boats make the transfer. The *San Francisco* was several hundred yards to port. The *Juneau* was about the same distance astern. I was casually walking with several of my shipmates, just looking and watching the transfer, when one of the men pointed to a periscope projecting some 5 feet out of the water, no more than 100 yards to starboard. We signaled to the bridge and pointed to the periscope. No action was taken, so we assumed it was one of our submarines.

A few moments later (11:09 AM), I started below to my living quarters. I was only a few steps down the ladder when I heard a tremendous explosion. I immediately retraced my steps. The *Juneau* had disappeared. Only a huge mushroom cloud of smoke remained. The *Juneau's* powder magazine had exploded like an atomic bomb when hit by a torpedo launched by the Japanese submarine SS-126. It probably was the same submarine we spotted a short time before.

Almost 700 men lost their lives when the *Juneua* exploded, including five brothers in the same family, the Sullivan brothers. Hollywood made a movie based on their lives a few months later. No search was made for survivors. I assumed there were none. Instead, we got underway fast and left the area.

One month later, we heard that about 50 men survived the sinking including one of the Sullivan brothers. Most of the survivors were wounded. They either died from their wounds, exposure, or eaten by sharks. Twelve men survived the ordeal and were rescued a week or so later.

The *Juneau* episode ended the most eventful and terrifying 24-hour period in my life. We had battled planes in the air, ships at sea, and were fired upon by a submarine.

The night engagement was a stand-off, with the edge going to the Japanese, insofar as losses of ships and men were concerned. However, when missions and objectives are considered, we won a resounding victory. We made mistakes that cost us dearly, but we prevented the Japanese from pounding our positions on Guadalcanal, their primary objective.

It was a battered, but proud Task Force that returned to Espirato Santos. As we led the *San Francisco* and the three destroyers past other ships in the harbor, they saluted and cheered. Another high moment in my life.

There were a number of messages praising our efforts. I was proudest of two statements made by top commanders at the scene. Admiral Halsey, Supreme Commander of Naval Forces in the South Pacific said," Your names will be written in letters of gold on the pages of history and you have won the undying gratitude of your countrymen. No honor for you would be too great; my pride in you is inexpressible."

A message from the Commanding General, First Marine Division, on Guadalcanal said it best, "...to Scott, Callaghan and their men, who, against seemingly hopeless odds, with magnificent courage, made success possible by driving back the first hostile attack, goes our greatest homage. In deepest admiration, the men on Guadalcanal to them lift our battered helmets".

Guadalcanal Engagement.
Damage to the *Helena*
during November 13 battle

Direct Hit on No. 4 Turret

Hit On Stack

Hit Main Deck

U.S.S. Helena

November 16, 1942

<u>MEMORANDUM TO ALL HANDS:</u>

Rear Admiral Turner, our Force Commander for the task just completed, has asked that the following be published to all hands:

1. "IN DISSOLVING TASK FORCE SIXTY SEVEN I EXPRESS THE WISH THAT THE NUMBER "67" IN THE FUTURE BE RESERVED FOR GROUPS OF SHIPS READY FOR AS HIGH PATRIOTIC ENDEAVOR AS YOU HAVE BEEN. ALTHOUGH WELL AWARE OF THE ODDS WHICH MIGHT BE AGAINST YOU I FELT THAT YOUR CHANCE OF NIGHT ATTACKS ON NOVEMBER 12 WAS THE TIME WHEN FINE SHIPS AND BRAVE MEN SHOULD BE CALLED UPON TO THEIR UTMOST. FOR YOUR MAGNIFICENT SUPPORT OF THE PROJECT OF REINFORCING OUR BRAVE TROUPS ON GUADALCANAL AND YOUR EAGERNESS TO BE THE KEEN EDGE OF THE SWORD THAT IS CUTTING THE THROAT OF THE ENEMY, I THANK YOU. IN TAKING FROM THE ENEMY A TOLL OF STRENGTH FAR GREATER THAN THAT WHICH YOU HAVE EXPENDED, YOU HAVE MORE THAN JUSTIFIED ANY EXPECTATIONS. FOR OUR LOST SHIPS WHOSE NAMES WILL BE ENSHRINED IN HISTORY AND FOR LONG CHERISHED COMRADES WHO WILL BE WITH US NO MORE, I GRIEVE WITH YOU. NO MEDALS HOWEVER HIGH CAN EVER POSSIBLY GIVE THE REWARD YOU DESERVE.

WITH ALL MY HEART I SAY "GOD BLESS THE COURAGE OF OUR MEN, DEAD OR ALIVE, OF TASK FORCE SIXTY SEVEN".

/s/ G. D. LINKE,
Commander, U.S. Navy
Executive Officer.

CL50/P15/MM

U.S.S. Helena

November 17, 1942.

MEMORANDUM TO ALL HANDS:

1. The following messages are quoted herewith for the information of All Hands:

MESSAGE FROM ADMIRAL HALSEY:

"TO THE SUPERB OFFICERS AND MEN WHO HAVE PERFORMED SUCH MAGNIFICENT FEATS FOR OUR NATION IN THE PAST WEEK. YOUR NAMES WILL BE WRITTEN IN LETTERS OF GOLD ON THE PAGES OF HISTORY AND YOU HAVE WON THE UNDYING GRATITUDE OF YOUR COUNTRYMEN. NO HONOR FOR YOU WOULD BE TOO GREAT; MY PRIDE IN YOU IS INEXPRESSABLE. TO THE GLORIOUS DEAD, HAIL HEROES, REST WITH GOD. GOD BLESS EACH AND EVERY ONE OF YOU. MAGNIFICENTLY DONE".

MESSAGE FROM ADMIRAL TISDAE:

"IF WORDS COULD ADD TO THE TRIBUTE PAID YOU BY THESE MEN OF CACTUS MY STAFF AND I WOULD JOIN ALL AMERICANS IN SAYING THEM. WE ARE PROUD TO BELONG TO THE SAME SERVICE WITH YOU".

MESSAGE FROM THE COMMANDING GENERAL, FIRST MARINE DIVISION

"IT IS OUR BELIEF THAT THE ENEMY HAS SUFFERED A CRUSHING DEFEAT. OUR THANKS FOR THE STURDY EFFORTS OF LEE LAST NIGHT, AND TO KINCAID FOR HIS INTERVENTION YESTERDAY. THE RELENTLESS POUNDING OF THE FOE BY OUR OWN AIRCRAFT HAS BEEN GRAND. WE APPRECIATE ALL THESE EFFORTS, BUT TO SCOTT, CALLAGHAN AND THEIR MEN WHO, AGAINST SEEMINGLY HOPELESS ODDS, WITH MAGNIFICENT COURAGE, MADE SUCCESS POSSIBLE BY DRIVING BACK THE FIRST HOSTILE ATTACK, GOES OUR GREATEST HOMAGE. IN DEEPEST ADMIRATION, THE MEN OF GUADALCANAL TO THEM LIFT THEIR BATTERED HELMETS".

MESSAGE FROM THE COMMANDING OFFICER, *U.S.S. PENSACOLA*:

"THE OFFICERS AND CREW OF THE *PENSACOLA* WISH TO EXPRESS TO YOU THEIR HEARTFELT ADMIRATION FOR YOUR HEROIC ACTION".

/s/ G. D. LINKE,
Commander, U.S. Navy,
Executive Officer.

On November 16, Admiral Turner, our Task Force Commander, dissolved Task Force 67. In his message, he closed with these words: "God bless the courage of our men, dead or alive, of Task Force 67."

After a few days in Santos, we headed south for repairs at Noumea, New Caledonia, the location of Admiral Halsey's headquarters. Shortly after we arrived, Admiral Halsey came aboard. We thought his purpose was to congratulate our skipper. Wrong!! Captain Hoover was relieved of his command on the spot! The crew was in a state of shock. Why??

No official explanation was given. We understood Admiral Halsey was enraged over Captain Hoover's handling of the *Juneau* episode. He thought Captain Hoover should have dispatched a destroyer to search for survivors. Years later, Admiral Halsey admitted he made a mistake.

Few words were spoken when Captain Hoover said goodbye. His departure left a void in each of our lives, not filled by his replacement, Captain Cecil, nor any Captain we served under during the remainder of the war.

I suppose you could classify the *Helena* crew as battle hardened veterans after our battle experiences. I am sure we had been hardened to a certain extent, but the fear was still there. Fear had become an ever present companion, almost from the first day we arrived in the South Pacific.

Many people believe battle hardened men are brave. They believe battle hardened men are daring and unafraid under fire. Few men, battle hardened or not, are unafraid in battle. Discipline, training, and experience cause men to do their duty under fire in spite of their fears. Men tested in battle may display more courage and bravery under fire than those who have not been tested, but the reason is not that they are unafraid of the dangers involved. They simply have better control over their fears.

The more I learned about living conditions our Marines had to endure on Guadalcanal, the more I appreciated living conditions aboard the *Helena*. Our Marines would go for days, sometimes weeks without a bath or changing into fresh clothing. Aboard the *Helena*, we had plenty of fresh water and a full size laundry. We could take a shower and change into fresh laundered clothing every day.

Rest was hard to come by ashore. Marine & Army men had to sleep in foxholes or make-shift tents with little protection from insects or the weather. As a consequence, casualties from tropical diseases ran high. Marine units lost 25 percent of their men to malaria alone. Insofar as navy men were concerned, we had a steel roof over our head and a comfortable bunk type bed, with freshly laundered covers, to sleep on. We had no problem with tropical diseases.

I don't suppose it makes much difference whether you are killed by the enemy ashore or at sea, but there is a big difference in how you are forced to live up to that point. I must admit, the Navy fought the war under the best living conditions possible for its men. My hat is off to the Marines and Army foot soldiers that fought under such filthy and unsanitary conditions.

Even with their losses and mission thwarted on the 12th and 13th, the Japanese continued to step-up the attack. On the 14th, they dispatched ten big transports southward with men and supplies. Our carrier based planes sank six, but four got through and unloaded their cargo on Guadalcanal.

On the night of November 14 and 15, two battleships and four destroyers tangled with a Japanese force made up of one battleship, four cruisers, and nine destroyers. They lost the Battleship *Kirishima*, the one we missed on the 12th and 13th. We lost two destroyers with one battleship and two destroyers damaged.

This action marked the end of the battle called "The Naval Battle of Guadalcanal" that started on the afternoon of the 12th. We did not know at the time, but this engagement proved to be the turning point in the war in the Pacific. From this point forward we were on the offensive.

Another night battle was fought on the night of November 30-December 1. A Tokyo Express made up of eight destroyers was intercepted by a vastly superior American force, consisting of five cruisers and six destroyers. We came out second best in this engagement. They lost only one destroyer while sinking one of our cruisers and heavily damaged three more that required almost 12 months to repair. Victory would not come cheap or easy.

The ground war was going badly for the Japanese on Guadalcanal. While the Japanese Navy fought brilliantly at sea, their troops ashore suffered one defeat after another. This was due primarily to the skill and bravery of our Marines, but their defeats were due in part by the poor or, you could say, stupid tactics employed by the Japanese field commanders.

The war was relatively quiet during December. We were again operating out of Espiritu Santos. Ironically, my four-year enlistment expired on December 13. I had originally planned to get out of the Navy at the end of four years and go to college. The war changed my plans. Congress had extended everyone's enlistment for the duration of the war.

The Japanese began to realize they were not going to take over Guadalcanal as originally planned. Supplying their troops with food, ammunition and other essential supplies became too costly and dangerous to maintain. On January 4, 1943, unknown to American Intelligence, the Japanese High Command decided to evacuate Guadalcanal.

That very night, actually 1:02AM on the 5th, the *Helena, Nashville*, and *St. Louis*, with two destroyers shelled Munda Airfield, located on the New Georgia Island. During a shore bombardment, only one ship fires at a time. I went topside to watch the other ships fire. I was particularly interested in watching the *St. Louis* fire, since she was a sister-ship with the same number and caliber of guns.

It was a fascinating sight. When the *St. Louis* opened fire, she appeared to be one huge ball of fire. You could see the shells leave the muzzle of the guns, go into a high arch, then disappear in darkness near the horizon. The stream of shells looked like sparks made by a piece of metal when placed against a spinning emery wheel. Someone remarked in jest that a fast welder could weld the shells into a bridge from the *St. Louis* or *Helena* to shore during the bombardment. In less than ten minutes we had fired 1,224 rounds of ammunition.

At 9:02 the same morning we were attacked, without warning, by six Japanese dive bombers. I was topside near one of our five-inch gun mounts when we opened fire. The noise and concussion from the guns firing damaged my ear drums. For several days I could hardly hear a sound. To this day, I have difficulty hearing certain sounds with my left ear. The New Zealand cruiser, *Achilles*, who had joined us only a short time before, was heavily damaged in the attack. Our formation shot down three of the enemy planes.

We participated in another night shore bombardment on January 24, at 2AM. Our target was Villa-Stanmore Airstrip on Kolombangara Island. We unloaded 1306 rounds of ammunition in this action. A short time later, about 3:30AM, our formation was attacked by several torpedo planes. Their torpedoes missed their targets. Insofar as could be determined, we failed to shoot down any of their planes during this attack.

In January, the Tokyo Express began to systematically remove all of the Japanese troops from Guadalcanal. American commanders were not aware they were removing men and supplies off the island until the evacuation was complete. This was probably the best kept secret of the war. On February 5-6, they completed the evacuation by removing more than 11,000 men from Guadalcanal.

Not until February 9, did our troops discover what had happened. That afternoon, the Commanding General on the island released this message: "Total and complete defeat of Japanese forces on Guadalcanal effected today, Tokyo Express no longer had terminus on Guadalcanal". We all breathed a sigh of relief. After six months of hard fighting we had turned the tide.

Few American or Japanese who fought there ever heard of Guadalcanal before our landing on August 7, 1942, but none of us would forget Guadalcanal or our experiences there.

The six months under combat conditions had begun to take its toll. The *Helena* crew was almost totally exhausted, both physically and mentally. I had lost 15 pounds since we left San Francisco (now about 145 pounds).

This was due in part to the heat. The temperature was continuously in the high 90's during the day. At night, it would drop to the low 80's or high 70's. Living spaces were not air conditioned. We would wake up after several hours in bed and find our mattresses saturated with perspiration.

Food was a factor also. We always had three meals a day, but there was a noticeable change in the menu after we arrived in the South Pacific. Instead of fresh milk we had powered milk. Practically everything we ate had been dehydrated before shipment to us. There was very little fresh meat, but plenty of canned peas and beans. Fresh fruits were in short supply and a real treat when available.

I'm sure our Commanders were well aware of the situation. Ordinarily, men are not required to stay on the battle front for extended periods of time. They were rotated periodically to a rest area for liberty and relaxation. When Captain Cecil announced that the *Helena* had been ordered to Sydney, Australia for three weeks, you cannot imagine a happier bunch of men.

We expected to be sent somewhere for rest and relaxation, but no one in their wildest dreams thought it would be Sydney. The atmosphere aboard ship changed immediately following the announcement. Everyone was in a festive mood. We were going to forget the war and have a good time.

In early March, shortly after sunrise, the *Helena* dropped anchor in the harbor at Sydney. The fog was so thick you could not see the shore. While waiting for the fog to lift, to allow us to proceed to a docking area, a motor launch arrived bringing fresh milk and fruit. I had forgotten how fresh milk tasted. It was the most delicious and refreshing drink I had ever tasted. I must have consumed a quart before the supply ran out.

The first liberty party, consisting of 50% of the crew, had lined up on the main deck ready to go ashore even before the lines were secured to the dock and gangway lowered. I was not one of the lucky ones to be in the first liberty party, so I watched with envy as they went ashore. They didn't walk off the *Helena*…they ran. They whooped and acted crazy as they disappeared from sight toward downtown Sydney.

The next morning we had first hand reports on liberty in Sydney. From all accounts, they had the prettiest girls, the friendliest people, and the best booze in the world. There was some truth to their stories because they reeked with the smell of perfume and alcohol.

At the time Australia was part of the British Commonwealth and subject to the British Crown. I soon discovered the "Aussies" (their nickname… they called us "Yanks") disliked the British even though they were fighting alongside them in the battle against the Axis powers.

Sydney is the largest city in Australia, with a population at the time of about two million, and comparable to American cities in almost every respect. Language was not a barrier. We got along beautifully. Hollywood movies had placed all Americans on a pedestal in their eyes. I doubt the feeling was as strong after our visit as it was before we arrived.

When liberty was given to my section, at noon the next day, we reacted the same way as the other section had as they headed for downtown Sydney. It was a great feeling. We roamed around Sydney in groups of two's and three's, but we always seemed to find ten or more shipmates at every stop. One of the finest restaurants in town was our first stop. We ordered the largest steak on the menu with all the trimmings. From this point on, it was bars (they called them pubs), night clubs, and dance halls. It was in the wee hours of the following morning before we returned to the *Helena*.

This routine was repeated every other day during our stay there. We were determined to make up in three weeks all the lost liberties in the previous nine months.

One of our special stops was a huge dance hall. It was a beautiful place, with two bands located on a circular revolving stage providing continuous music. When one band stopped playing the other band would be rotated into view. Of course the main attraction was the 100 or so single girls who were always in attendance.

During the last week of our stay, the political leaders of Sydney treated the crew and their dates to a dinner and dance at one of the nicest clubs in town. I attended both nights. The first night I was part of a Shore Patrol Detail, assigned to maintain order at the party. There were no problems during the dinner. As the evening progressed, the bottles of Scotch and other types of booze at every table began to have its effect. By 11PM, with one-half of the crew in attendance, the place was so noisy you could hardly talk to anyone without shouting.

The most amusing incident of the evening occurred at about this time. As I passed the Officer-in-Charge of our detail, on one of my rounds through the crowd; he directed my attention to a sailor near the entrance to the dance hall. He was making amorous advances to one of the girls at the hat check counter. The officer said," Get him out of here and send him back to the ship".

The officer did not know it, but he was my brother, Roy. He offered no resistance as I placed him on an elevator. I instructed him to catch a cab back to the *Helena*.

Fifteen minutes later, the Officer-in-Charge stopped me and pointed in the direction of the hat check counter. "I told you to get that sailor out of here!"

I looked and saw he was right. This sailor was back with the girls. When I asked him why he came back, he just smiled. This time I placed him on the elevator and waited for the elevator to return from the first floor. When the door opened, there he was wearing a sheepish grin. There was only one solution. I placed him in custody of a shipmate returning to the *Helena*. He did not return, but I would not have been surprised if he had.

The last day of our three week stay came too quickly. The *Helena* was needed in the drive northward from Guadalcanal.

We left Sydney with many fond memories and hopes of returning in a few months. We had no way of knowing then, but the *Helena* and many of its crew would not be returning to Sydney or anywhere else for liberty. In less than four months, the *Helena* with 168 members of her crew would be at the bottom of the Kula Gulf.

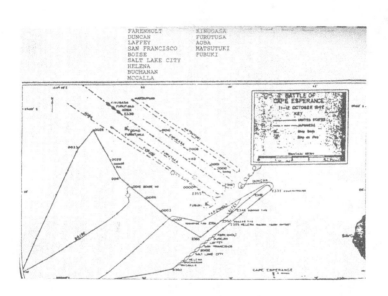

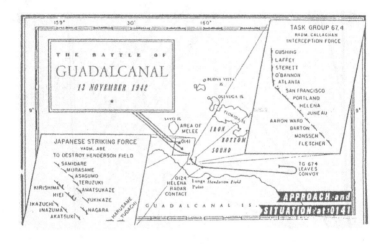

NAVY YEARS....

HELENA GOES DOWN IN KULA GULF APRIL - SEPTEMBER, 1943

While we were enjoying liberty in Sydney, the war continued without let-up. The Japanese were beefing up their defenses north of Guadalcanal. We began to step up our air and sea attacks on enemy positions in preparation for a landing on the New Georgia Island where the Munda airfield was located.

Although I enjoyed every minute of our stay in Sydney, it had very little impact upon a change in my mental attitude which had been building for months. I began to realize I had experienced enough combat to last a lifetime. The constant stress and strain was beginning to have an effect upon my frame of mind. Gone was the desire to be where the action was. Rather there was a stronger feeling to get as far from combat as possible.

There were times each day when you could relax to a limited degree. For example, there were movies each night. Every day or so we would exchange films with other ships. Consequently, there were always several good movies on hand for showing.

Several of us in the E-Division had chipped in and purchased a record player before we left San Francisco. Oftentimes at night several members of our Division would gather in the I C Room (one of the few air conditioned spaces on the *Helena*) to listen to music by Glenn Miller, Harry James, Benny Goodman, and other top band leaders of the day. Of course there was no television. In addition, we were too far away from the States for good radio reception. There were short wave news broadcasts, but little otherwise. Occasionally we would listen to "Tokyo Rose", a propaganda program from Japan for laughs.

I suppose the best source of entertainment was gambling. There were several poker games going every night. For those who wanted faster action, there were Black Jack and Dice games. There were "penny-ante" games to no limit stakes.

Although I played it all, poker was the only game I was able to come out ahead most of the time. My gambling investment was limited to $15 each pay day. The remainder of my salary (about $80 per month) was sent home by allotment check for mother and dad to place in a savings account for me.

During this period the most popular gambling game among members of the E-Division was Pinochle. We played with a double deck which provided four of each card, nine and above. We seldom played partners, always "cut throat", with every man for himself. Even though we played for a penny a point, you could run up some big scores and lose $10 to $15 a night if your luck was real bad. Generally, though, losses or winnings were limited to less than $5 per session.

Pinochle was not a good game for me financially, but overall gambling possibly netted me $200 to $300 during our stay in the South Pacific. Non-gambling games were popular too. The two I enjoyed the most were Cribbage and Acey Ducey.

About this time, a few men in our Division began to receive orders back to the States for specialized training and other duties. Of course, there were plenty of applicants for any opportunity to be transferred back home.

I thought my name would be high on the list of those eligible for transfer. I had been in rate (First Class Petty Officer) for over 18 months with almost no hope of advancement. We had a full complement of Chief Petty Officers. There had to be a vacancy at that level before any First Class could advance. The chances of this happening were remote.

I talked to the officer in charge of the E-Division, about a transfer. He let me know in a hurry that he had only been aboard three months. He knew very little about the Division or its operation. He was not about to let his most experienced men go anywhere. If I insisted and submitted a request for transfer, he would make sure it was disapproved. Knowing any further action would be fruitless, I abandoned all hopes of leaving the Helena through normal transfer procedures.

On May 13 at 1 AM, the *Helena, Honolulu, Nashville,* and five destroyers shelled the Vila Airstrip on Kolombangara Island. At the same time, three mine-laying destroyers mined the Bairoko Harbor on the New Georgia Island less than 10 miles away. The *Helena* fired over 1,200 rounds of ammunition in this operation.

On June 30, American troops landed upon Rendova Island as part of a campaign to take over Munda Airfield, which was being used by the Japanese to raid our positions on Guadalcanal and Tulagi.

The Japanese reacted by sending troops to Vila by destroyer transport. From here, they were transported by barge and landing craft across Kula Gulf to the fighting front on the New Georgia Island.

At 12:25 AM on July 5, the *Helena, Honolulu, St. Louis* and four destroyers shelled Vila Airstrip and Bairoko Harbor again in an attempt to wreck the Japanese supply system to that area. We lost one ship, the destroyer *Strong,* when she hit a mine and sank. The *Helena* fired about 1400 rounds of ammunition in this action.

The very next night we were ordered back into Kula Gulf to intercept a destroyer transport group believed to be heading for Vila. At 1:40AM on July 6, radar picked up the enemy task force made up of ten Japanese destroyers.

During this engagement, my battle station was located at the Aft Repair Station near #4 Turret just below the main deck.

At 1:54AM, we opened fire. The flashes from guns firing at night made the ships in our task force a perfect target for enemy guns. Under Captain Hoover we would fire for short periods of time, pause, then fire again. The Hoover tactics permitted us to maneuver to another position by the time the enemy had our range and bearing. In addition, the pauses gave our lookouts a better chance to spot incoming torpedoes, thereby giving the Captain an opportunity to change course if necessary.

Captain Cecil had a different tactic. He believed firing without let-up was best as long as there was a target within range. We had been firing for about five minutes continuously when radar reported several enemy ships were maneuvering in such a way as to indicate they were launching torpedoes in our direction. We continued to fire.

At 2:01AM, a torpedo struck our bow between #1 and #2 turrets. We stopped firing almost immediately.

Roy was stationed at the Forward Repair Station located just below the main deck by #2 Turret. He said later, the water rushed into his battle station so fast, following the explosion, that he had to almost swim to reach a safer spot some fifty feet aft of his battle station.

We learned later that the torpedo explosion had completely severed 120 feet of the bow from the rest of the ship. Roy was lucky. The separation was made just forward of the compartment where his battle station was located. Ironically the bow continued to float. Our own ships sank the bow with Number 50 clearly visible, several hours after the battle.

Back where we were, everything was relatively calm. We knew we had been hit by a torpedo. The ship slowed down, but the *Helena* remained on an even keel. No one thought there was cause for alarm. After all, the *Helena* had been hit by a torpedo before.

We expected to be called upon to help make temporary repairs as soon as the extent of damages was known. We anxiously waited for the damage reports to come in.

We did not have to wait long. Less than 60 seconds after the first torpedo struck we were hit by a second to be followed a few seconds later by a third. The second and third torpedo hit the Forward Engine and Forward Fire Rooms almost ripping the *Helena* apart near her mid-section. The *Helena* was virtually broken into three pieces.

After the second and third torpedo explosions, the *Helena* began to slowly tilt forward and to starboard. There was no panic. Men began to move about asking questions about the damage and what we should do. Someone asked if we should abandon ship, but few thought the damage that serious.

A few minutes later, men began to arrive at our Damage Control Unit from battle stations below. We waited for orders. Some seconds later-seemed like hours-Commander Cook (Engineering Officer) who was stationed below in the Aft Engine Room, stopped on his way topside and told us to abandon ship. This was it! Abandon ship? Surely not the *Helena*, but it was happening.

The hatches topside were opened. We quickly made our way to the main deck. By the time I reached the main deck, the bow section was completely under water up to the Quarter Deck with the ship tilted forward. The "Fan Tail" (rear section) was completely out of the water on the port side. There was about a 25 degree list (tilt) to starboard. The water was no more than two or three feet below the main deck on the starboard side where I stood... whereas normally it was 15 to 20 feet.

It was a strange sight. In the darkness of the night, I could see hundreds of lights scattered over a wide area around the ship. Every man, who had abandoned ship, had a flash light as part of their battle gear. The strange lights were coming from these flashlights that had been shorted out by the salt water.

I could see guns flashing in the distance, so I knew the battle was still in progress.

I stood several minutes assessing the situation. All the life rafts had been launched and were approximately 100 yards from the *Helena*. There was no panic. Men were not jumping-they didn't have to-they simply stepped over the starboard side of the *Helena* into the water.

I hesitated about getting into the water. Somehow I believed the *Helena* would stay afloat. I could not bring myself to believe the *Helena* was sinking. She had been my home for almost four years. I did not want to abandon her unless there was no hope. By now I was one of less than 50 men aboard.

About this time, I began to hear a loud snapping, popping, and grinding sound coming from the area where the two torpedoes had hit. I looked in the direction of the noise. I could see that the forward section of the *Helena* had assumed a different angle than the rear section. The forward portion was heavier and taking on water faster, therefore it was sinking at a faster rate than the rear section where I stood. The noise was caused by heavy steel plates being twisted and pulled apart. The two sections were about to separate completely.

Now I knew the end was near. I started to step over the side when I discovered I had not inflated my life jacket. The life jackets we had were much like an automobile inner tube. They had to be inflated with lung power. Later versions could be inflated simply by pulling a cord that released air from a miniature C02 canister.

While I was inflating my life jacket around my waist, a young kid, who had just reported aboard, no more than 17 years old, asked if he could tag along. Of course, "just follow me". I could tell he was terrified. Frankly, I was too. I told him we would swim to the nearest raft that could be seen about 100 yards away. We both stepped off the *Helena* and started to swim toward the raft.

We must have been in the water two or three minutes when I looked back and discovered we were making very little headway. The suction of the water entering the *Helena* was pulling us back about as fast as were going forward.

If there was a time, during this ordeal, that I almost panicked, this was it. I had heard stories of men being sucked under when they were too close to their ship when it went down.

I hesitated a moment to figure out what to do next. I could tell it was too dangerous to continue swimming at a right angle away from the *Helena*. Then I noticed that although we were no more than 15 or 20 feet from the *Helena*, the current of the water had taken us about the same distance further aft toward the stern. We were close to a 45 degree angle from the point where we had entered the water.

My brain raced. I gambled that our best bet was to swim at the same angle, 45 degrees, as the ocean current, suction of the ship, and our swimming effort was moving our bodies. It worked! A short time later we were a comfortable distance from the *Helena*. In a few minutes we were alongside a raft. The raft was already filled to capacity, so we joined about ten other men hanging on the ropes along the side of the raft.

A few minutes later, as we were catching our breath from the swim, one of the men inside the raft shouted and pointed in the direction of the *Helena*. We were no more than two - three hundred yards from the *Helena* at the time. I looked and the forward section of the ship, including the bridge superstructure, was slipping underwater at a 15 to 20 degree angle. In less than 10 seconds the entire section disappeared from view leaving the stern portion afloat but tilted forward at about a 25 degree angle. We knew it would only be a question of minutes before the stern section would go under too.

Fortunately, the water was calm and warm so we didn't experience any physical discomforts from weather conditions. However, I was sick at my stomach from swallowing salt water mixed with fuel oil. The torpedoes had ruptured several boiler fuel tanks spreading thousands of gallons of heavy black oil several inches thick over a wide area around the *Helena*. Of course our entire body, from head to toe, was covered with oil.

What do you think about under these circumstances? My first thoughts were about my brother Roy and his safety. But, there was nothing I could do except pray he was okay. Otherwise, I thought about being rescued and my physical well-being.

There was the possibility of being hit by shell fire. Although the battle was miles away, judging from the gun flashes on the horizon, there was no way of knowing if the fight would return our way or not. In addition to being hit by shell fire, we could be run over by our own or enemy ships. I don't know why, but I thought about submarines and depth charges. I had heard of men being ripped apart internally when a depth charge exploded nearby. Of course, I thought about sharks.

I wondered how the battle was going. If we were victorious, we could expect to be picked up soon by one of our ships. However, if we were losing, we would be at the mercy of the elements and the Japanese.

I could see a mountain jutting out of the ocean in the distance. I knew the island was controlled by the Japanese, so landing there would mean imprisonment or worse.

Believe it or not, I thought about 30 days leave at home. In recent weeks a new Navy policy had been announced with regard to survivors. No longer would survivors be reassigned to ships in the area. Instead, each survivor would automatically receive 30 days leave in the States before being reassigned to another ship or station. All I had to do is make sure I was a survivor!

Notwithstanding all my thoughts and worries, there was one over-riding conviction; I realized how helpless I was in determining my own fate. There had to be a supreme being in control of life. Whether or not Roy, my shipmates or I made it was in His hands. So I prayed...

Even though we had many other things on our minds, everyone kept their eyes riveted on the stern section of the *Helena* as it tilted more and more forward. It is an agonizing experience to watch any ship die, but it is especially traumatic when the ship is one you love and had become an important part of your life. As we watched, the stern section nosed over and assumed a perfect vertical position. With spray shooting high into the air she quickly disappeared from view. Even in death she was graceful.

Everyone holding on outside the rafts was able to get aboard after a second and third raft were tied together. What a relief! Although my feet were in the water, I could at least sit down to rest.

As we paddled toward the island, we began to come in contact with other rafts. Within an hour we had six rafts tied together with about 75 men aboard. We believed there was safety in numbers. Also, the larger the group the better our chances of being spotted by our ships and planes.

Between 3:30 and 4:00AM, we spotted a ship several miles away. It was moving slowly in one direction-then another. At one point, it disappeared from view, and then returned 10 to 15 minutes later.

We hesitated about making our presence known. In the darkness we could not determine if it was friend or foe. All we could see was a dim profile of a ship. If it was Japanese, we were in real trouble.

Finally, after some anxious waiting, the ship began to send a message by signal light to another ship (we could not see) over the horizon. There was a signalman aboard our raft who could read the Morse code message being sent. When he announced that it was an American ship we started shouting and waving our arms to attract their attention.

A short time later, one of the ship's motor whale boats came alongside. The boat was too small to carry all of us in one trip, so it was decided to tow the rafts to the ship. As though we didn't have enough problems, the tow line got tangled around the propeller of the boat as they were trying to connect the rope to the rafts.

It took about 15 minutes to free the propeller-seemed like hours. Finally the rope was freed and we began to make our way to the ship about a mile away. It was now about 5AM., almost daylight. We soon discovered the ship was the *Nicholas*, one of our newest destroyers. We quickly climbed aboard. What a relief to stand on a dry surface again!!

For the first time I noticed how filthy and grimy we were. Oil had saturated our clothes. It was in our hair, blackened our face, and covered our entire body from head to toe. We were a sight to behold!! We looked so unreal that I didn't recognize a single one of my shipmates. Even the kid I left the ship with was just another grimy face in the crowd. In fact, I never saw or heard from him after we left the raft. Our first thought was to get rid of the filth and grime. Members of the *Nicholas* crew led us to one of the ship's shower rooms. Most of us had removed our clothing preparing to enter the shower when the General Alarm sounded. Over the public address system, the *Nicholas* Captain announced that radar had picked-up incoming Japanese planes.

My heart went out to about 100 men, in the water near the *Nicholas*, when the Captain told them he had to leave. But, he assured them he would return and pick them up as soon as possible. Following this announcement, he signaled the engine room for flank speed. Soon we were moving at speeds in excess of 40 knots, about 50MPH.

Within a short period of time, the *Nicholas* began firing at the Jap planes. Their 5" guns were not equipped with hydraulic lifts to carry shells from storage areas to the guns. Instead, they had to use a chain of men to pass shells from one man to the next until the shells reached the guns. In no time, the *Helena* survivors were a part of the ammunition chain alongside the *Nicholas* crew. It is impossible to picture the scene... naked, greasy, grimy figures, intermingled with clean, fully-clothed men passing ammunition.

The air attack lasted only a few minutes. Apparently the Japs were only interested in surveying the battle area looking for ships damaged in the battle or possibly trying to locate Japanese survivors.

The *Helena* was the only ship our task force lost or damaged in the battle. The Japanese lost two destroyers sunk, one destroyer heavily damaged, and four destroyers received minor damage.

The *Helena* fired over 800 rounds of ammunition before being torpedoed. At the time, the *Helena* had fired more rounds of ammunition, in enemy action, than any ship in the history of the navy. The total number of five and six inch rounds fired, in enemy action, totaled over 10,000.

On December 20, 1944, the Navy made the first award of the newly created NAVY UNIT CITATION to the *Helena*. The citation said in part, "For outstanding heroism in action against the enemy. The *Helena* opened the night BATTLE OF CAPE ESPERENCE, sinking a hostile destroyer. She engaged at close quarters a superior force, in the BATTLE OF GUADALCANAL, rallying our forces, contributing to the enemy's defeat. In her final engagement, her guns blazing aided in the destruction of an enemy force before being struck by Japanese torpedoes." (I consider it an honor to have served on the *Helena*)

In less than three hours after our rescue, we were in Tulagi Harbor (across the channel from Guadalcanal) being transferred to the light cruiser *Honolulu*. The *Nicholas* crew could not have been nicer to us. Even though we outnumbered them, they gave us food, clothing, and helped us get rid of the dirt and grime. The *Nicholas* was a mess when we disembarked. I was so grateful that I pledged to name my first son Nicholas to honor this gallant ship and crew.

Two days later we landed at Espirato Santos. One of the first men I saw was George Baddour, a long-time friend of the family, from Covington. He was assigned to an Army unit based there.

The *Helena* survivors totaling about 475 men were assigned quarters with a Navy Construction Battalion (Seabee's) located only a short distance from the docking area. For three weeks I lived in a Quonset Hut (metal semicircle top building) with 75 other men.

One of my first acts ashore was to send a telegram home to let mother and dad know I was safe. Ordinarily, the Navy waited a week or more before announcing the names of ships sunk in battle. But, in this instance, they mentioned the *Helena* had been sunk when accounts of the battle were released to the news media. The mental anguish mother and dad experienced must have been tremendous. The cablegram arrived in Tipton County about a week after the sinking.

While this relieved half of their worry, they still had not heard from Roy. I tried through Navy sources at Santos to determine if Roy had been rescued. They could or would not tell me anything. Several survivors remembered seeing him leave the *Helena*, so I knew he was not wounded and probably among those picked up later.

Weeks later, I learned that Roy was within inches of climbing aboard the *Nicholas* when the Japanese planes attacked. He said he thought about trying to grab the cargo net draped over the side, but was afraid his hands were too greasy to hold on. Had he been able to get his hands on the net and not been able to hold on, there was a good possibility he would have been crushed by the ship's propellers. He was almost too close anyway... he said he could have touched the propeller guard as the *Nicholas* passed by.

Three motor whale boats, left behind by the two destroyers in the rescue operation, spent the entire day towing the 88 men in Roy's group to a small Jap-held island. They spent the next night on the island. In the early morning hours of the next day, they were rescued by two destroyers and taken to a rest camp in Noumea.

There was a second group of nearly 200 men not rescued the night the *Helena* went down. They spent the next two days and two nights at sea before landing on Vella Lavella Island. They spent nine days on the Japanese infested island, being cared for by natives and coastwatchers. Of the original group, 165 men survived the 11-day ordeal. They were picked up by destroyers and taken to Noumea and quartered with Roy's group.

Our stay in Santos was uneventful. Everyone was anxiously awaiting orders back to the States for a 30-day vacation. I spent several days with George Baddour discussing the war and home folks.

I thought the food was especially good, even though our Seabee buddies complained about having "Spam" (a brand of luncheon meat) too frequently. Spam was not a part of our diet on the *Helena*. I loved the stuff. They served it three meals a day. They fried it, baked it, and mixed it with other food items. I remember one noon meal, they had fried Spam, spaghetti mixed with slices of Spam, and beans with chopped up Spam.

The Salvation Army was there and furnished survivors with clothing and other basic needs. If the Red Cross was there, they did not make their presence known. Even though I have always held this against the Red Cross, I contribute to their fund raising drive each year. In contrast, I give to the Salvation Army willingly and more generously.

During the first week in August, we received orders to report to Treasure Island, California, for 30 days leave and reassignment. There could not have been a happier bunch of men as we boarded Amphibious Personnel Carriers (nicknamed "Ducks") for the trip to a merchant ship, anchored in the harbor that was preparing to get underway for a trip to the states.

The mood was temporarily broken by an incident that occurred as we were attempting to go aboard the merchant ship. When we pulled alongside, one of the ship's officers ordered one of his men to lower the gangway for us to come on board. To everyone's surprise, the seaman replied, "Not unless you pay me double-time!" The officer did not agree to pay overtime. The gangway was not lowered. We had to climb aboard using cargo nets that were hanging over the side of the ship. I am sure we would have beaten that seaman to a pulp had we been able to get our hands on him at the time.

The ship was named the "Lew Wallace" one of the hundreds of "Liberty Ships" produced during the war to transport men and supplies to the battle fronts across the Atlantic and Pacific. We soon discovered these ships did not have many of the extras we had taken for granted on the *Helena*.

They did not have a laundry for passengers. To wash clothes we would tie our shirts, pants, etc. to the end of a rope. We would then tie the other end of the rope to the main deck of the ship. Finally we would drop the clothes in the water to drag alongside the ship. The friction and pounding of the clothes in the water acted like a washing machine. The only danger was in leaving the clothes in the water too long. Several forgot to pull their clothes out of the water after an hour or so and retrieved only a few shreds of cloth that were previously shirts and pants.

We didn't have fresh water for bathing or shaving. I tried to bathe in salt water, but gave up after several attempts. Soap, not even "salt water" soap, would lather in salt water. Several hours after bathing, you could see salt flakes over your entire body. As a consequence, I did not have a real bath during the entire trip.

I do not believe it possible to shave using salt water alone. Although it was strictly prohibited, I did "borrow" fresh water from a drinking fountain to shave several times before we arrived in San Francisco.

Movies were shown every afternoon and evening. One problem, they had only three selections. Only one, Casablanca, carried a top rating. Since they were shown in my sleeping quarters, I watched Casablanca several times and listened to it a dozen times or more during our 30-day voyage. Ingrid Bergman and Humphrey Bogart were great in this one. I can still hear her say "Play it Sam" and remember the song Sam played, "As Time Goes By".

We were strictly passengers with little to do except keep our quarters clean. The Captain of the ship was a real "rube". He would announce over the P.A. System, "prepare for daily inspection", "keep spaces in apple pie order".

There were plenty of gambling opportunities during those early days out of Santos. I had about $15 when we left Santos. My bank roll didn't last long in a game of "Red Dog". In this game, the banker (one of the ship's officers) would deal each player four cards. Each player would then bet he had a higher card, in suit, than the next card the dealer exposed from the deck. The game is heavily loaded in favor of the banker.

Finally, late one afternoon during the first week in September, we sailed under the Golden Gate Bridge and docked at the end of Market Street in San Francisco. We had been gone 14 months, but it seemed a lifetime.

Shortly after we arrived, sacks and sacks of mail were delivered. The Post Office had held our mail in San Francisco following the news of the *Helena* sinking. I had not received a letter from home in over two months. There were about 30 letters for me to read. Those from mother and dad were the most touching and heart-breaking letters I have ever read. Tears streamed down my face as I read several of them.

One of dad's (he never wrote, mother did all the writing) really got to me. He wrote, after hearing of the *Helena* sinking, "We prayed that at least one of our boys would survive, but after hearing from you, we wanted Roy safe too". In one of his more recent letters they had heard from Roy. He was safe! What a relief!

Next day we were transferred for processing and reassignment to Treasure Island. The first thing I did, after checking-in, was to take a long hot shower and then shave. I had almost forgotten how it felt to be clean. Next I called home. I asked dad to send $200 by Western Union. I was flat broke. Our pay records were messed-up. I needed the money for pocket change and to purchase a train ticket home.

While waiting on the money to arrive, I borrowed $10 from a shipmate. I spent all but $1 in a barber shop for a shave (my first in a barber shop), shampoo (another first), and haircut. I felt like a human being again. Although I was anxious to go home, I was concerned about my next assignment. Whereas, 18 months before I wanted combat duty, this time I was hoping for shore duty or a non-combat ship operating in the "boon docks" as far away from the war as possible. However, my wishes ran contrary to Navy thinking at the time. Reassignments were generally made ship to ship not ship to shore. Even worse, from my point of view, reassignments were made from one combat ship to another combat ship.

Within a week, most of the *Helena* survivors, including myself, had orders 'to report on or before October 15 to the *U.S.S. Hornet*, a new aircraft carrier under construction at the Newport News Ship Yards near Norfolk, Virginia.

Good News! At least the ship was located on the East Coast. I thought it would take at least a year…possibly longer… before the *Hornet* would be ready for combat in the Pacific. I was wrong. The *Hornet* would join the Pacific fleet at Majuro

Atoll (in the central Pacific) on March 20, 1944. But, for now, my only thoughts were about my upcoming thirty days leave in Tennessee.

Bill Jim Davis

The islands of New Georgia, Kolombangara, and Rendova, below, showing the importance of the Kula Gulf and the relative battle area.

Postal Telegraph

MHA2   EFM CABLE VIA IMP=AMISRO NIL=
MR JESSE R DAVIS=
         =RT2 (STANTONTENN) (ELEVEN)=

ALL WELL AND SAFE PLEASE DONT WORRY LOVE=

   =W K DAVIS.

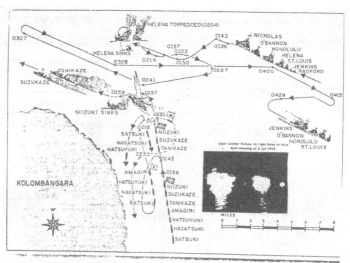

A simplified track chart of the Battle of Kula Gulf showing the course and approximate times of action for the opposing forces, 6 July 1943.

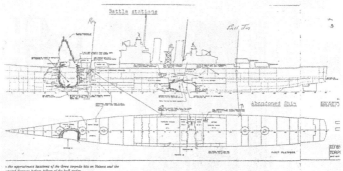

Battle stations

Roy

Bill Jim

Abandoned Ship

the approximate locations of the three torpedo hits on Helena and the
several damage before failure of the hull girder.

This drawing (from Navy Sources) shows the torpedo hits that sank the HELENA in 1943

The first torpedo severed 120 feet of the bow from the ship which floated for hours after the
remainder of the HELENA sank.

The second and third torpedoes broke the ship in the middle with the forward section sinking first
followed a short time later by the rear portion which assumed a vertical position before
disappearing beneath the surface.

The top drawing shows Roy & my battle stations when the torpedoes hit. The bottom drawing shows
where we abandoned ship.

The Covington Leader, Wednesday, May 24, 1989   ****   Page A9

IN HONOR OF AMERICA'S FINEST

U.S.S. HELENA

U.S.S. Helena

During World War II Bill Jim Davis and Rob Roy Davis, brothers, were assigned to the U.S.S.
Helena. The ship was engaged in several major naval battles in the South Pacific. It was damaged
by a torpedo at Pearl Harbor on Dec. 7, 1941. It was struck by three torpedos on July 6, 1943, and
sunk. The Davis brothers survived the Pearl Harbor attack and were onboard when the ship was
sunk. Both escaped without injury.

U.S.S. Hornet

Bill Jim Davis served aboard the U.S.S. Hornet, a huge aircraft carrier, in the South Pacific during the latter part of World War II. Davis and his brother, Rob Roy Davis, were serving on the light cruiser, U.S.S. Helena, when it was sunk by Japanese torpedoes in 1943.

Roy and Bill Jim Davis home on leave March, 1942. Aboard
USS Helena at Pearl Harbor December 7, 1941. The *Helena*
was torpedoed four minutes after the attack started…killing 21
and injuring 79. Roy and Bill Jim were not injured.

Graduating Class- General Motors Diesel School
Flint, Michigan..October 1944

Bill Jim Davis

Above: The USS Helena suffers torpedo wounds, but her antiaircraft guns slow down six Japanese planes. Right: Destroyers Downes and Cassin with flagship USS Pennsylvania in rear.
Below: Sent to neutral countries for propaganda purposes, this aerial photograph shows Hickam Field aflame in the distance.

106

U. S. S. Helena CL-50

Compliments Jess King

Pearl Harbor

Battleship Pennsylvania

Cruiser Helena

SAFE ABOARD THE RESCUE SHIP, THESE SURVIVORS OF CRUISER "HELENA" POSE FOR A HAPPY GROUP PHOTOGRAPH. THOUGH HAGGARD, THE MEN WERE IN GOOD SHAPE

"HELENA" RESCUE

Navy snatches cruiser survivors right from under noses of Japs

Some Jap officers in the South Pacific must have caught holy Nipponese hell last month when their superiors learned that the U. S. Navy had brazenly sailed into Jap-held territory, landed on a Jap-held island and taken off 161 Americans who, by all rights, should have been Jap prisoners. The Americans were men of the U. S. Cruiser *Helena* which had gone down in the Kula Gulf battle on July 6 after helping sink five Jap warships. Most of the *Helena*'s crew had been picked up in the Gulf. But these 161 had

drifted to Vella Lavella, an island well inside Jap area.

U. S. planes spotted them and the Navy decided to take the chance of rescuing them. A flotilla of destroyers and destroyer-transports sneaked through to Vella Lavella. It was a risky job. The landing boats got stuck on sand bars. The destroyers had to wait offshore on a moonlit sea. But no Japs interfered. The boats came back with the rescued and the flotilla sped home. On the expedition was William Shrout, LIFE photographer, who took these pictures.

One of the first USS Helena reunions

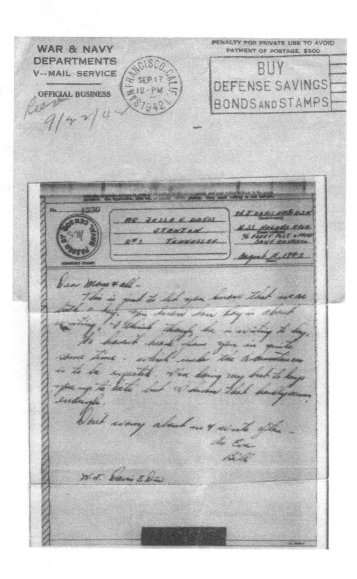

Helen and Bill Jim Davis at opening of Tipton County
Veteran's Memorial in Covington, TN (1998)

USS HORNET SEPTEMBER-1943 AUGUST-1944

Only military men know the joy, the peace, and the feeling of thanksgiving that come when you first greet your family at home, after an extended period of time in combat. The tears I shed were not so much the joy of seeing loved ones, as it was in thanksgiving for having been spared injury or death when hundreds of my shipmates had not been so lucky. I had never experienced this feeling before. Even my home coming after Pearl Harbor was different. My experience there was of short duration-not enough time to fully soak in. But, 14 months of constant stress, strain, and tension had saturated my entire being. Without realizing it, I was both physically and mentally exhausted. During this period, there was much rejoicing in the Davis household and the Charleston community. Roy was on his way home and expected home in about two weeks.

Due to publicity given the *Helena* sinking and our rescue, my homecoming was given front page coverage in the Covington Leader. I was treated like a hero everywhere I went. I never felt comfortable-I'm sure Roy felt the same-when anyone spoke of my experiences in this light. I had not performed any heroic deeds. I had merely done my duty in a combat situation. My observation has always been, "heroes are made in the minds of the observer rather than the participant".

My entire leave was spent on the move from early morning to late at night. Mother made a special effort to prepare meals she knew I liked. I enjoyed spending an hour or so each day dad's store talking to customers and friends. Joy and Shirley were proud of their big brother and close by most of the time. The trading of the family automobile was one special happening during my stay. Everything was rationed during the war... sugar, gas, tires, etc. No new cars were being manufactured, except for military use. However, new car dealers were still in business doing mostly repair work and selling or trading an occasional used car.

Everett McCormick, salesman from Walker Chevrolet Company in Covington, had been trying to trade cars with dad for some time without success. I had been home about a week when he came by with a 1941 Fleetline Chevrolet that had been used as a demonstrator. It was loaded with extras… radio, heater, even a knob on the steering wheel for easier steering. Without a doubt the prettiest car I had ever seen.

Dad did not want to trade because he thought the $600 trading price was too much. He reasoned our 1938 Chevrolet had not cost much more than the $600 difference. It was only after I insisted and agreed to pay the difference did he agree to trade. I got about as much enjoyment in driving the car as I did anything else during the remainder of my leave.

Roy came home one week before I had to leave for Newport News, Virginia. Having us both at home, safe and sound, was surely the most memorable occasion in mother and dad's life. They were so proud and thankful. Roy and I were together almost constantly during my last days at home. We had a "ball". For the first time I became aware that people, outside the Charleston community, thought we were twins. Our names Bill Jim and Rob Roy, plus our war experiences together, must have implanted this idea in their minds. The same belief persists to this day.

Following my departure, Roy stayed on another two weeks before having to report to the *Houston*, a new cruiser under construction at Newport News, Virginia. We would no longer be serving on the same ship. The loss of the five Sullivan brothers aboard the *Juneau* was responsible for changing the Navy's policy of allowing brothers to serve together. At least we would be together for a few more months, since the *Houston* & *Hornet* were under construction at the same shipyard.

Newport News, Virginia, was a city of about 30,000 population at the time. The shipyard was their only big industry.

The shipyard was one of the oldest-started in about 1890, and one of the largest in the country, employing approximately 14,000 men and women. During World War II, this privately owned yard built 350 ships from the smallest to the largest afloat.

We had always operated in and out of government-owned shipyards. They were usually dirty and loosely run operations-indicating a lack of pride in their work and their employer. While the civil service employees were skilled in their trade, it usually took two or three to do a one-man job.

The first thing I noticed about the Newport News yard was its cleanliness. It was almost spotless. Their workers were not only skilled and efficient, but kept busy from the beginning to the end of each shift.

Although I had serious misgivings about going back into combat, I was glad I had been assigned to an aircraft carrier. If I had to go, there was no better assignment in the navy than the *Hornet*, or so I thought at the time.

The *Hornet* was one of the largest and most powerful of its type in service during this period. She weighed 33,000 tons, over three times the weight of the *Helena*. The flight deck was about 1,000 feet long, towering some 75 feet above the waterline.

The *Hornet* was designed to handle about 90 warplanes almost evenly divided between fighters, dive bombers, and torpedo planes. The number of men assigned to man the ship and planes totaled some 3,500 men, over four times the number aboard the *Helena*.

There are three distinct groupings of men aboard a carrier. In addition to ships company, there is is an aviation department in charge of flight operations, and when planes are aboard there is an air group consisting of pilots, crews members, and mechanics.

The *Hornet* was about 99 percent complete when I reported aboard. Instead of being quartered aboard the ship, we lived in barracks nearby and walked to and from our work station aboard the *Hornet* each day.

I was part of a "pre-commissioning" detail, composed of about 500 men. Our job was to work with yard workers so we could learn as much about the ship, its equipment and machinery, before the Navy took over.

The first day I reported aboard I met with the Officer-in-Charge of the Electrical Division. He outlined the various areas of responsibility open to me. When he mentioned he wanted to place me in charge of the automatic telephone system, I quickly accepted. This would be a challenging experience for me. We had an automatic telephone dial system aboard the *Helena*, but I knew absolutely nothing about the equipment. I looked upon it as a golden opportunity to learn a trade that could be helpful in getting a job with the telephone company after the war was over.

I immediately went to work with a Western Electric Company representative who was in charge of installing the telephone equipment. During the next few weeks I spent hours each day going over blueprints, circuits, and manuals, trying to learn as much as possible about the equipment before the ship was commissioned and ready to join the Pacific Fleet.

My work station and later my battle station, was the Telephone Exchange located in an air-conditioned space called the Interior Communications (I C) room. The space is at the bottom of the ship, some 12 levels (approximately 100 feet), below the flight deck. There was not a more comfortable place on the ship to work. In addition I was convinced there was not a better work assignment within the Electrical Department.

There were some 600 dial phones aboard the *Hornet* to be serviced and maintained plus the exchange equipment. The dial phones were no different than regular dial phones in civilian homes. Tracing the electrical circuits from the impulses generated when you dial a number through selectors, connectors, switches and contacts to the phone you dialed was fascinating.

Newport News was not a good liberty town. There were several restaurants and beer "joints" we visited during the week. But, on the week-ends, we headed for Washington, D.C. about 190 miles away.

Our nation's Capitol was not only attractive because of its many fine restaurants, night clubs, and hotels but, primarily because the boy-girl ratio was three to one in favor of the girls. War-related jobs had brought women into Washington by the tens of thousands. Many had civilian jobs, but there were as many, if not more, in uniform, WAVES, WACS, WRENS, etc. Needless to say, we had some wild week-ends in Washington.

Since none of us owned an automobile, we would hitch-hike to and from Washington. This, however, didn't prove to be a handicap. We were required to be in uniform on and off the base. (I wouldn't have worn civilian clothes even if permitted...I was proud to be in uniform). In those days only a few cars would pass before one would stop and offer to take those in uniform to the next town. Some would even go out of their way to take us closer to our destination or drop us off on a busier highway so it would be easier to get another ride.

There were exceptions... late one Sunday afternoon on the outskirts of Washington, two shipmates and I were on the main highway (now I 95) trying to hitch-hike to Richmond, Virginia. Richmond, about 100 miles from Washington, was the half-way point to Newport News. It was usually easier to get a ride to Richmond, then move to another highway to catch a ride back to Newport News.

Past experience had made us too confident, possibly a little cocky, about folks stopping to give us a ride. This day we decided not to accept just any offer. It had to be a late model car.

We turned down about a half dozen rides for this reason. Somehow the drivers must have sensed what we were doing and no longer stopped. They just passed us by. After about an hour of waiting we decided to change our tactics, we would accept the next offer regardless of the condition or age of the vehicle.

The next car was a 1938 Essex. The driver was a nice guy, but talkative and somewhat of a braggart. He had just purchased the car and was on his way to Richmond.

He let us know that the purchase of the car was not a snap decision. He had shopped around several weeks before deciding to purchase the Essex. He was not about to let a used car salesman take advantage of him. Not only was the car in good mechanical condition, but it had four new re-cap tires. He had driven such a hard bargain that the dealer had to fill-up the tank with gas. The tires and gas were real important because both were heavily rationed and in short supply in those days.

We were no more than 20 miles out of Washington before we began to notice the car was having difficulty making it up long grades without changing gears. By the time we had gone another ten miles, we were going down each hill as fast as possible in order to have enough momentum, plus changing gears, to make it up the next hill.

It was hilarious! We would pass everything on the road going downhill. Then watch the same cars pass us in the right lane as we struggled to make it to the crest of the next hill.

When we were about halfway to Richmond, the right rear tire blew. When he opened the car trunk preparing to change tires, he discovered there was no jack. We were lucky. The driver's brother-in-law, who had taken the driver to Washington, was following us back to Richmond. We borrowed the brother-in-laws jack. About this time we discovered the spare tire was flat. Now it would be necessary to patch the inner tube in the flat tire.

I can still see the driver reach inside the tire to pull out the inner tube. Instead of a tube he had a handful of rubber bits, none any larger than a dime. The tube, because of age, had disintegrated into a million pieces. We almost laughed out loud. Here again, he had to impose upon his brother-in-law who loaned him the spare on his vehicle.

We had gone no more than five miles down the road from the scene of the blow out when we ran out of gas. The driver would not believe we were out of gas. Not only had the dealer filled the tank before we left Washington, but the gas gauge showed the tank was 3/4 full. Either the dealer had not filled the tank or we had burned about 15 gallons of gas since we left Washington. Luckily, a small grocery store was about 1/2 mile down the highway. We had difficulty trying to keep from laughing as the driver purchased five gallons of gas.

At this time, we were beginning to think we would never reach Richmond without walking or catching another ride. The car's maximum speed, from the scene of the blow out, was no more than 20 mph. Now it was necessary to shift to the lowest gear just to make it over the slightest incline. Finally the car sputtered and quit near the city limits of Richmond. It had taken us about six hours to travel approximately 100 miles. The driver got into the car with his brother-in-law and left the Essex on the side of the road.

When they were out of sight, the three of us rolled in the grass for about five minutes, laughing about our experiences. I am certain, those passing by, thought we had lost our minds. A short time later a tractor-trailer rig gave us a ride to Newport News.

The *Hornet* was commissioned on November 29, 1943. The commissioning ceremonies were not too impressive to me at the time. I was one of the 1500 or so who had to stand at attention during the speaking and other formalities involved when the Navy officially places a ship into service.

Originally the *Hornet* was supposed to be named the *Kersarge*, but the ship was renamed after the loss of the first aircraft carrier named the *Hornet* in the South Pacific on October 26, 1943.

Our skipper was Captain Miles Browning, formerly Chief of Staff to Admiral Spruance in the Battle of Midway, where he proved to be a great strategist. However, we soon learned that he was quick-tempered and hell-bent upon getting back into the battle still raging in the Pacific.

Within two weeks we were in the Atlantic for sea trials. It brought back memories of the *Helena* sea trial. The weather was stormy. Winds from 50 to 75 mph pushed waves over the flight deck. But, the sheer size of the *Hornet* prevented the *Hornet* from pitching and rolling like the *Helena*. As a consequence only a few men were sea sick during those few days at sea.

In January, we had been completely outfitted and at sea off Bermuda for shakedown training. Planes were brought aboard to familiarize our flight deck crew with the machinery, equipment, and procedures necessary for flight operations.

I was topside at every opportunity to watch planes being launched and brought back aboard. The landing operation was particularly fascinating.

To land, planes would form a circular pattern around the stern of the *Hornet*. As each plane approached the stern for a landing, the Signal Officer would guide each plane, left-right, up-down using flag signals.

If the plane was not in the right position for landing or coming in too fast, it would be "waved off" to try again. Landing was a difficult maneuver for most pilots with only the most skilled able to land on the first try. Some would try two or three times before landing safely. Sometimes one of the pilots would try and try so many times that you began to think gunfire would be the only way to bring it down.

When everything was right, the plane would glide for a short distance over the flight deck with its tail hook down. When low enough the hook would catch one of the heavy cables stretched across the deck spaced about ten feet apart. The "arresting" cables, connected to hydraulic equipment below deck, would bring the plane to a complete stop in less than 50 feet.

As soon as the plane stopped, two men would race from opposite sides of the flight deck to disengage the tail hook from the cable. The pilot would then activate mechanism to return the hook to its normal position inside the plane.

At the same time, the pilot would start folding the wings of the plane as he taxied forward. Usually the planes would be spotted on the forward portion of the flight deck until all planes were landed. On occasions, some would be taken below by elevator to the hanger deck.

When all planes were safely aboard, they would be respotted on the stern portion of the flight deck and readied for the next flight operation. There were very few accidents during launching operations, but there were many accidents while planes were being brought aboard. During my tour aboard the *Hornet*, we lost at least 25 to 30 planes through accidents during landing operations.

We were back in port for the Christmas holidays. Our Executive Officer announced we would be leaving for the west coast, enroute to the Central Pacific, shortly after the first of the year. During this period, the entire crew, divided into shifts, would be given a four-day pass.

I spent the entire four days in Washington. I was having such a good time that I missed the last bus that would have taken us back to the *Hornet* before the 8AM deadline the next day. In desperation, I joined six of my shipmates in hiring a taxi for the return trip.

We left around 3AM. The speed limit was 35 mph. Although we tried to get the driver to go faster, so we wouldn't be late, he refused. Instead, we averaged less than 30 mph. We reported aboard 1 hour and 15 minutes late.

A few days later, I along with about 400 other shipmates, were ordered to appear at Captain's Mast for disciplinary action. We were all given the same sentence-three weeks restrictions. This was my first and last time to be charged with breaking any Navy regulations or orders.

As it turned out, the sentence proved to be almost no punishment. The infraction did not go on our record. We left Norfolk on February 14 and were at sea enroute to San Diego via the Panama Canal most of the three weeks.

We were in San Diego less than ten days. I recall going ashore the last day before departure for the war zone. Nothing unusual about the liberty, but remember how difficult it was to go back aboard the *Hornet* knowing the dangers ahead. This is when duty, honor, and country come into play. You do what must be done even though serious injury or worse may be the consequence.

After a brief stop-over at Pearl Harbor, we joined the fleet at Majuro Atoll in the Central Pacific on March 20, 1944. Since the *Helena* sinking in July 1943, American offensive efforts had expanded and accelerated throughout the Pacific. In addition to moving northward from Guadalcanal, capturing Vella Lavella and Bougainville Islands in the process, our forces began to move toward the Islands of Guam and Saipan in the central Pacific. Army and Marine amphibious forces supported by carrier task forces had captured the Gilbert and Marshall Islands before we arrived.

Life aboard an aircraft carrier is entirely different from duty aboard any other type of combat ship. Everything centers around flight operations with guns secondary. My nerves were on edge while the *Helena* was in a combat zone, but tension aboard the *Helena* was nothing compared to the stress and strain aboard the *Hornet* during combat operations.

During combat, the ship becomes a beehive of activity. Planes are not only landing and taking off, but they had to be refueled and rearmed. It was an especially dangerous time.

Rockets, bombs, and torpedoes were scattered everywhere from the flight deck to the ammunition magazines near the ship's bottom. There were accidents of one kind or another almost daily.

One day a fighter plane tipped over on its nose while landing. A piece of metal from the spinning propeller hit a marine standing on the catwalk alongside the flight deck. No more than six to eight inches of his head was above flight deck level, yet a sliver of metal hit the young man in the forehead, killing him instantly. After this accident, no one was allowed to stand on the catwalk during flight operations.

Following almost every bombing and strafing mission, planes would return with bombs and rockets still in place under their wings. Frequently, the jolt of landing would jar one loose and the rocket or bomb would sail down the flight deck. Usually the bomb or rocket would stop on the flight deck and be tossed over the side.

However, on one occasion a dive bomber (SB2C) made a rough landing. A 250 pound bomb fell off; hit the deck bounced 15 to 20 feet in the air. The spin type fuse rotated just enough revolutions to arm the bomb.

When the bomb hit the deck it exploded. Shrapnel hit one of the two men trying to disconnect the tail hook in the stomach area, almost ripping him apart, killing him instantly. The other man was hit in the hip area. Both legs had to be amputated.

I watched the explosion from the bridge area, above the flight deck. One man, no more than 10 feet from where I stood, was hit in the head and killed instantly. The explosion of the bomb opened a huge hole in the flight deck, killing one man and injuring three others on the hanger deck below. Altogether, five men were killed and 15 wounded.

Life was different in other ways aboard the *Hornet*. The number of men aboard totaled 3500, almost four times the complement of the *Helena*.

As a consequence, there was not the closeness or friendliness I found aboard the *Helena*. I knew almost everyone aboard the *Helena* on a first name basis. On the *Hornet* I was only close to the men in the Electrical Division. The ship was so spacious that every duty station seemed to isolate small groups of men from everyone else aboard.

As with any large group of men, it was difficult for those in charge to keep track of everyone. While I was aboard, a number of men simply disappeared during the night at sea. Apparently they fell overboard moving from one place to another along dark catwalks going to their work or battle station.

The daily routine was different. Simply feeding 3500 men was a monumental task. We ate in shifts. Men were in a chow line from early morning to late at night.

Recreation was much the same. There was gambling and movies. However, gambling was different. The Chief Master-At-Arms shut down all of the small gambling operations he could locate. There was a reason, other than the strict enforcement of anti-gambling regulations, he operated a casino (dice, Roulette, the whole bit) just below the flight deck. The Master-At-Arms and his staff must have made thousands on this operation.

My gambling activities were limited to an occasional game of Black Jack and Poker in the I C room. I tried to learn how to play Contract Bridge. Two "obliging" shipmates suggested we play for a penny a "just to make it interesting". It was a costly lesson. My partner and I lost $35 each the first evening. We continued to play bridge off and on, but without the gambling incentive.

In addition to the pressure of combat activities, I was getting depressed over my promotion status. I was long overdue for promotion. I had held the rate of first class petty officer for over 2 1/2 years. While my status was at a stand-still, the Navy was recruiting men as first class petty officers direct from civilian life. It didn't seem fair.

About the time I had almost given up on any promotion, things began to happen. When we arrived in the Pacific, the Navy announced a new policy. The new directive authorized Navy Commanders to recommend first class petty officers for promotion to Warrant Officer. This rank is between Chief Petty Officer...the highest enlisted rating-and Ensign-the lowest Commissioned Officer rank in the Navy. My name, along with two other first class petty officers, and two chiefs were submitted by Captain Browning to Washington for consideration. The announcement that I had been recommended for promotion was a real shot in the arm to my morale. Attaining warrant status is one of the most coveted goals of any enlisted man. Warrant Officer's wear the same uniform as commissioned officers. The pay was about the same as that of an Ensign. In addition-you would remain in your field of specialization. In my case I would continue to work with electricians. Also important, especially at the time, was the knowledge that I would be transferred off the *Hornet* if the recommendation was acted upon favorably.

While waiting for the recommendation to be acted upon (which I had doubts would be acted upon favorably because of being AWOL the one hour and 15 minutes before we left Newport News) two Chief Electrician's Mates were transferred to other ships creating two vacancies. I, along with several other first class petty officers, was examined for promotion. I was both happy and relieved when it was announced that I was one of the two successful candidates. The promotion took effect on May 1, 1944. It was an advancement in more ways than one. I moved into the Chief's Quarters. All Chief Petty Officers in the Navy are assigned spaces separate and apart from the other enlisted men. No longer did I eat cafeteria-style, instead mess cooks brought our food to the table. It was like moving into a country club compared with what I had become accustomed to. The bunks were larger, more comfortable, and not jammed together like they were in the regular enlisted quarters.

There was an increase in pay to about $135 a month. Another difference was the uniform. No longer did I wear bell-bottomed trousers, slip-over blouses, pea-coats and sailor hats. Instead, the Chief's uniform is identical to that worn by a Commissioned Officer. I was a happy man and almost forgot about the recommendation pending for Warrant Officer.

The advancement also resulted in a new job assignment. I was relieved of my duties over the Automatic Telephone equipment and placed in charge of all the electrical systems on the flight deck. To become knowledgeable about all the various specialized electrical equipment used in flight operations was another learning experience.

Now I was on the flight deck all the time except while eating or sleeping. My flight quarters and battle station was on the Bridge in the compartment where the Public Address equipment was located. I liked the assignment better because I could see everything that was going on. It was a nerve-racking experience to be sealed in steel compartments below deck, during combat conditions.

Shortly after becoming a Chief Petty Officer, I witnessed an incident that today I find difficult to believe happened. Understandably, it was not publicized. It was another one of those crazy episodes brought about by the stress and tensions on the minds and bodies of those in combat.

The Pacific Fleet was anchored at the Eniwetok Atoll in the Central Pacific. The Task Force was one of the most powerful ever assembled in one place. There were six other fleet carriers the size of the *Hornet*, about eight light carriers built upon *Helena* type cruiser hull, plus numerous battleships, cruisers and destroyers.

The incident occurred on the hanger deck while the crew was watching a movie. There were at least 1,000 to 1,500 men in attendance. A variety of chairs and benches were used to sit on with officers seated nearest the screen, enlisted men in the rear and Chief Petty Officers in the middle.

The picture was a war film. It was a good movie ("A Guy Named Joe") starring Spencer Tracy and Van Johnson. During one of those silent suspenseful portions of the movie, when you could have heard a pin drop, it happened. I heard a hissing sound coming from the rear where the enlisted men were seated. It sounded exactly like someone had lit a fuse to set off dynamite. Almost simultaneously, there was the sound of men moving around in the same vicinity.

Then someone yelled a bomb was about to explode. Pandemonium broke loose. The men in the rear started forward, running, jumping and stumbling over men and chairs as they raced away from the hissing sound. It was a stampede!

I stood my ground in the middle, undecided whether to join the stampeding herd or simply try to get out of the way. I was about to act when the main thrust of the crowd veered to my right to the side of the ship.

When the leading edge of the mass reached the edge of the ship, some 25 to 30 men jumped overboard. Then there was a pause, then silence for suddenly they realized there was no danger. As quickly as the stampede started it ended. The hissing sound turned out to be CO_2 gas escaping from a fire extinguisher. An enlisted man had accidentally activated the extinguisher while watching the movie.

Captain Browning quickly grabbed a microphone in the projection booth. Was he mad?! He called us everything but fighting men. The men were humiliated and embarrassed. The Captain's remarks only made a tragic occurrence worse. The unbelievable incident cost the lives of two men by drowning with about 15 men with broken arms and legs.

June 10, 1944, was one of the most memorable days of my life. On this date, a message was received from the Navy Department in Washington with information about the five men recommended by the Captain to the rank of Warrent Electrician.

Four months had passed since the original letter had been submitted. I thought the papers had been lost, or the long delay could mean the recommendation was disapproved. Actually, I was almost sure the proposal would be disapproved. The odds were too great to hope for favorable consideration. Also, I was enjoying my new promotion and had almost forgotten about the recommendation.

One of the Chief Petty Officer's recommendations was disapproved. Two First Class and one Chief were approved for promotion to Warrant Electrician. When the Personnel Office told me the action taken upon my recommendation, I could not believe my ears. They said I had orders to report to San Francisco to be COMMISSIONED AN ENSIGN!! (date of rank from March 17, 1944) and for further assignment!!

Another one of those high moments in my life. It was almost unheard of for the Navy to authorize a promotion in excess of the recommendation by a field commander. Some of my closest shipmates said I must have used political influence to obtain such a prized promotion.

Of course, the suggestion was not true. To this day, I do not know why my recommendation was given such a high rating. I was only a high school graduate. Insofar as anyone knew, you had to have at least two years of college to become a Commissioned Officer. The only explanation that makes any sense was my age. Twenty-three was rather young to be a Warrant Officer, but about the right age for Ensign. Of course, I like to think it was the recommendation itself which was given in recognition of my performance of duties assigned to me.

During those early months aboard the *Hornet*, I was relatively content with the assignment. The daily routine during our stay on the East Coast was almost like shore duty. There was even a certain amount of "glamour" to the assignment.

The Aircraft Carrier had replaced the Battleship as the most important ship in the Navy's arsenal.

But, duty aboard an Aircraft Carrier in the battle zone was anything but "glamorous". The war in the Pacific had virtually become an air war. This statement should not take anything away from the Marine and Army units who had to take and hold the real estate involved. But it was clearly evident at this time that the side controlling the air above the battlefield would win the war.

As a result, fast Carrier Task Forces were spearheading every advance in the Pacific. Not only was the carrier the center of activity during every offensive action, but the prime target of the enemy.

I always felt, even in battle, a certain degree of safety aboard the *Helena*. I never had this feeling aboard the *Hornet*. There was too much hustle and bustle, too many accidents of one kind or the other for comfort. Possibly my experiences aboard the *Helena* were responsible, for I expected the worst to happen every time we put out to sea.

The *Hornet* was on the move almost from the moment we joined the Pacific Fleet. On April 20, we provided air support for the invasion of New Guinea. Later we participated in massive air raids against Japanese bases in the Carolina Islands.

On June 11, one day after I learned of my promotion to Ensign, our planes were raiding Tinian and Saipan in preparation for an amphibious assault upon Saipan scheduled for June 15. The following day we were attacking Japanese bases on Rota and Guam

On June 15 and 16, our planes were blasting enemy air fields at Iwo and Chichi Jima to prevent enemy air attacks upon our troops invading Saipan. You cannot imagine the anxiety I experienced during this period. With orders to return to the States by the "first available transportation" yet in the middle of one of the most decisive battles of the war.

About this time, American Submarines reported a strong Japanese carrier task force was heading our way with orders (we later learned) to annihilate the U.S. Pacific Fleet in one decisive battle. Their fleet was made up of nine carriers, five battleships, 13 cruisers and 28 destroyers. The number of planes they had at their disposal was 430 Carrier based planes and about 100 more land-based planes on Guam, Rota and Yap.

To meet the enemy attack, American Commanders had assembled a naval force superior in almost every category. The fleet consisted of seven fleet and eight light carriers for a total of 15 carriers, seven battleships, 21 cruisers and 69 destroyers. The number of planes we had at our disposal totaled 891 -- all carrier based.

The American battle force was divided into five separate units spread out over a 25-mile radius. It was an awe-inspiring sight with ships as far as the eye could see. Our particular unit consisted of two fleet carriers (*Hornet* and *Yorktown*), two light carriers (*Belleau Wood* and *Bataan*), and 11 destroyers. The unit was under the command of Rear Admiral J.J. (Jocko) Clark, part Cherokee Indian, with headquarters aboard the *Hornet*. The entire fleet was under the command of Admiral Spruance, with headquarters aboard the cruiser *Indianapolis*.

On June 18, our Fleet was about 150 miles west of Tinian with the Japanese Fleet some 400 miles further west in the Philippine Sea. The Japanese Commander planned to attack at the 300 mile range because their planes could operate at this distance while our planes could not operate much beyond 200 miles from their carriers.

The main battle was started at 10 a.m. on the 19th when the first of four waves of enemy planes were spotted by radar about 150 miles away. Fighter planes were launched and they destroyed 40 planes before they could reach their target. One plane scored a direct hit on the battleship *South Dakota*, but none got through to our carriers. The sky was filled with anti-aircraft fire. Of the 60 planes in the first Japanese raid, only 24 survived.

The second wave of 130 planes came in a short time later. Fighter planes prevented all but about 50 from reaching the target area. While about 25 planes tangled with our screening force, the rest headed for the carriers. Less than a dozen got through only to be knocked down by gun fire.

I watched the whole show from my perch on the second level of the superstructure above the flight deck. During the entire battle, only one enemy plane came close to the *Hornet*. The plane, after being hit by gunfire, spun out of control, barely missing the flight deck. Only 32 planes in the second wave returned safely.

The third wave of 47 planes never reached the target area. Enemy reports indicate they were not able to find our position. All but a few returned safely to their carriers.

The fourth wave missed our position also. One small group of about ten planes attacked one of our carriers. They did no damage. All but one was shot down. The rest headed for Guam to refuel. Before they arrived, they were jumped by about 30 of our fighter planes (Hell Cats F6F's) which shot down about 50 of their number. Most of the remainder crash-landed on Guam. Only nine planes of the 82 returned to their carriers.

The "Battle of the Philippine Sea" proved to be the greatest carrier battle of the war. Our fighter pilots referred to the battle as the "Great Marianas Turkey Shoot" for they shot down over 300 planes that day. In addition to plane losses, the Japanese lost two carriers when their fleet was attacked by two American Submarines. Our victory was so complete that Japanese carrier units never again ventured out of port to challenge our war efforts in the Pacific.

After recovering our planes late in the evening on the 19th, we headed west in search of the enemy fleet. It was not until late afternoon on the 20th did our search planes report the Japanese position about 275 miles away.

Even though our Commanders knew it would be after dark before our planes could return from a strike at this distance, the decision was made to launch an all-out effort. In less than 15 minutes, over 200 planes from ten carriers were launched.

Our planes reached the enemy fleet position at about 6:45 p.m. They sank one carrier, two tankers and damaged several other ships before breaking off the engagement. We lost 20 planes in the attack.

Our planes started to return at about 9 p.m. The night was pitch-black. You could hear the planes buzzing around and spot them by the fire from their engine exhausts. All I could see of the *Hornet* from my battle station was the dim outline of the flight deck below.

Each carrier was equipped with landing lights. But they proved to be of little value to the pilot trying to locate a carrier because they were only visible when the plane was at the right altitude in its landing approach.

It was an eerie spectacle. All the planes were running out of gas. They had no time to locate the right carrier or wait for routine landing instructions. Instead they took matters into their own hands and tried to land when and wherever they could.

Of the dozen or so planes which attempted to land on the *Hornet*, only one landed safely. The rest crash landed. The pilots were saved, but the planes were damaged so severely that they were pushed over the side into the ocean.

After about 30 minutes of this nightmare, orders were given to turn on all lights topside including searchlights to make recovery easier. The lights from ten carriers piercing the darkness looked like some 4th of July fireworks display.

Less than 1/2 of the returning aircraft landed safely with most of those on the wrong carrier. Altogether, over 100 planes were lost from crashes and ditching into the ocean by the pilot when they ran out of gas.

We gave up the chase on June 22, and returned a few days later to Eniwetok for fuel, supplies and replace the planes lost in battle.

As soon as the *Hornet* dropped anchor, we (those with promotions to Officer status) started working on Personnel to locate some kind of transportation back to the States-- anything -- we were not choosey. Two days passed and nothing happened. I was miserable. The *Hornet* was scheduled to get underway on the 28th. If we were not transferred before we weighed anchor, it would be days - possible weeks - before the *Hornet* returned to port.

When almost all hope was gone, just a few hours before the *Hornet's* scheduled departure, we received orders to report to the Battleship *Maryland*, which was enroute to Pearl Harbor. I was a happy man.

As the motor whale boat pulled away from the *Hornet*, I felt the anxiety and tension which had been building up over the past few months subside. There was a little sadness, too, for the *Hornet* had been good to me. Fate had placed me on the right ship at the right time. My future was never brighter. I wonder even today what my future would have been like had I been assigned any ship in the Navy other than the *Hornet*.

After a short lay-over at Pearl Harbor, I caught a ride on a Transport heading for the West Coast. During the first week in August, I reported to the Commandant Twelfth Naval District located on Treasure Island just across the bay from San Francisco. This was the beginning of a new phase in my life. I would be commissioned a Naval Officer on August 10.

A year before I was very concerned about my next duty assignment. This time I was so proud of my new status that I looked forward to the next assignment, confident it would be to my liking.

NOTE: The stampede on the hanger deck resulted in Captain Browning being relieved of his command of the *Hornet* on May 29, 1944.

Bill Jim Davis

Pers-639-sbj-36
NN 295 44 31

Navy Department
BUREAU OF NAVAL PERSONNEL
WASHINGTON 25, D.C.

14 April 1944

<u>AIR MAIL</u>

<u>R E S T R I C T E D</u>

From: Chief of Naval Personnel

To: CO, U.S.S. HORNET

Subj: DAVIS, William James, EM1c, U.S.N., (Successful Candidate for
Commission); transfer of.

1. Please transfer subject man to ComTwelve furaspers.

2. ComTwelve inform BuPers (Pers 31547) date of availability.

By direction of Chief of Naval Personnel:

J.T. TALBERT
Captain, U.S. Navy
Director, Enlisted Distribution Division

CC:
CNO (Op-32)
ComTwelve
ComServPacSuberComd

COMMISSIONING CEREMONY

*

The Commandant accepts the ship from Newport News Shipbuilding and Dry Dock Company. Mr. Roger Williams, Executive Vice President, will represent the company.

Commandant requests permission of the Secretary of the Navy to proceed with the commissioning.

The Commandant refers to the commissioning directive.

The Commandant orders, "Sound Colors".

Marine Guard presents arms, Division Officers bring divisions to "Hand Salute", band plays National Anthem. National Ensign, Jack, and Commission Pennant are hoisted together.

Commission Pennant is lowered, the Flag of the Secretary of the Navy is hoisted, and honors rendered.

The Chaplain gives invocation.

The Commandant turns ship over to the Commanding Officer,

The Commanding Officer reads his orders and accepts the ship.

The Commanding Officer directs the Executive Officer to "Set the Watch". Boatswain pipes and sings out, "Set the Watch, first Section". Division Boatswain's Mates will pass the word from forward aft on the flight deck. Navigator takes the first watch as Officer-of-the-deck.

The Navigator reports to the Executive Officer that Watch has been set.

The Executive Officer reports to the Commanding Officer that Watch has been set.

The Commanding Officer introduces Mrs. Frank Knox, sponsor of the ship.

The Commanding Officer introduces the Secretary of the Navy.

The Secretary of the Navy makes address.

Presentations of any awards or citations.

The Commanding Officer orders, "Pipe Down".

Men will remain in ranks until Retreat is sounded.

U. S. S. HORNET

*

KEEL LAID 3 AUGUST, 1942

SHIP LAUNCHED 30 AUGUST, 1943

SPONSOR, MRS. FRANK KNOX

COMMISSIONED 29 NOVEMBER, 1943

―――――――

REAR ADMIRAL D. M. LE BRETON, U. S. N.
Commandant Fifth Naval District

CAPTAIN MILES BROWNING, U. S. N.
Commanding Officer

LST 343
AUGUST, 1944 - JUNE, 1945

My promotion to Ensign was one of the most important milestones in my life. Without a doubt the promotion had a profound impact upon my future in the Navy, not only during the remainder of the war, but beyond.

The promotion would have been most welcome under any circumstances, but I was especially proud because I had worked my way up through the enlisted ranks. Navy men referred to officers in this category as "Mustangs". In numbers they made up less than 5% of the officers in the Navy.

There were no formal commissioning ceremonies. The offer of a temporary promotion had been made. After being found physically fit, I merely signed papers accepting the appointment. That was it.

Immediately following the paper signing, I headed for a clothing store in San Francisco that specialized in Navy officer's uniforms. Other than several tropical khaki uniforms that could be adapted by changing insignia to my officer wardrobe, I had to be completely outfitted. Next to the Marines, I thought the Navy officer's uniform was the best looking in the armed forces.

Ordinarily, I was conservative in my uniform purchases, but in this instance I spared no expense. I picked the finest material, gold braid, and accessories. I wanted the best. Even for the combat ribbons, that were ordinarily pinned on, were sewn in place because they looked neater and were easier to keep clean.

There may not be much truth in the statement "the clothes make the man", but they make you feel better and give you a better outlook on life. In any event, wearing the officer's uniform sure gave my ego a lift. The opportunities for the future seemed to be endless at the time.

I had no official duties while waiting orders to a new duty station. As I waited, there was plenty of time for relaxation and liberty in San Francisco.

I love this city. To the Navy man it is one of the best liberty ports in the United States. Even today, I would pick San Francisco for a fun vacation over any other city in the world. It has everything - perfect climate, it is a gathering place for every nationality in the world, there is Chinatown, Fisherman's Wharf, trolley cars, Golden Gate Bridge, the ocean, plus some of the finest restaurants and theatres to be found anywhere.

My stay on Treasure Island was of short duration. On August 22, I received orders to report to the Amphibious Engineers School, located in Flint, Michigan, for a six-week course.

I arrived in Flint on August 26th. There were no quarters available for officers, so I checked into the Flint Tavern Hotel. This was the beginning of one of the most fantastic six-week periods of my life.

Flint was a city of about 100,000 population located about 60 miles north of Detroit. Before the war, it was one of the largest automobile manufacturing cities in the nation. During the war, it turned out tanks and other instruments of war.

Being the only military personnel within a 50 mile radius made Flint a fabulous duty station. Even better from my viewpoint, the detachment was small, totaling less than 100 men. The people, especially the female portion, could not be nice enough. We were showered with attention everywhere we went.

The purpose of the school I attended was to teach future engineering officers as much as possible about the various diesel engines used by the Navy in its Amphibious Fleet. The school was one of the best the Navy had to offer and operated under contract by the General Motor Corporation.

There was much to learn. Unfortunately, I didn't learn as much as I should have. There was supposed to be some home study work. But there was too much going on after school hours to spend any time on lessons for the next day.

From the moment I checked in until I departed, I did not average sleeping three hours a night. I lost so much sleep that I could not relax enough to sleep in bed. Unfortunately, I found it easy to doze off in class. On one occasion, toward the end of the course, I actually dozed off standing up while an instructor was showing us how to operate a diesel engine. I would have hit the floor had not a fellow officer caught me.

Obviously, I was enjoying to the fullest my new officer status, which explains my over-indulgence in night life activities. As an enlisted man I had not given much thought to the subject, but an officer is much more highly respected by the general public than those holding enlisted status. I was now welcome in the most exclusive private clubs. As an enlisted man I was not. As a result, I found myself going to nicer and more expensive places than before.

The difference was possibly a carry-over from conditions which exist aboard each ship or station. An officer has nicer quarters, better prepared food and generally better working assignments than the enlisted man. Military regulations require enlisted men to respect all officers. As evidence of this respect, they are required to carry out every command without question and give a hand salute when approaching the officer.

One of the principle reasons officers were more respected by the general public was possibly due to the fact they were seldom involved in "brawls" and generally better behaved ashore than their enlisted counterpart. The type of place each group frequented had much to do with their behavior. Another factor was the higher standards used by the military service in the selection of officers over those used in the selection of enlisted personnel. All in all, the enlisted man is more relaxed and has more fun ashore than the officer.

I completed the engineering course with passing grades during the first week in October. About one week later, on October 9, I was detached with orders to report to the Amphibious Base at Coronado near San Diego, California, for reassignment.

Since there was a delay in reporting to October 21, I detoured through Tennessee for a few days at home. The family was about as pleased with my promotion to Ensign as I was.

The war news was encouraging. American forces were advancing on all fronts. It was obvious at this point victory would be ours. The only question was how soon.

Just before leaving for the West Coast, we learned the *Houston* had been torpedoed by Japanese planes off Formosa on October 14th. Roy was safe. Later he told of his experiences. It made for an interesting story.

The ship was operating in heavy seas when attacked. They received only one torpedo hit, but it exploded in the keel section flooding most of the engineering spaces. Some of the men, thinking the ship was going to sink, abandoned ship without orders. Others waited for orders to abandon ship before going over the side. Finally there were only about 150 men and the Captain left aboard. I am sure the fact that most of the crew were survivors of the *Helena* sinking was a factor in so many leaving the *Houston* without clear-cut orders to do so.

After about an hour in the water, Roy was picked up by a destroyer, later transferred to a cruiser and then to a tanker which carried him to Ulithi, our advance base in the Central Pacific. Here they discovered the *Houston* was still afloat and being towed to Ulithi. Without waiting for the *Houston* to arrive, Navy officials ordered all former crew members to Pearl Harbor for further assignment.

Shortly after their arrival at Pearl Harbor, all Petty Officers were ordered back to the *Houston*. A short time later, Roy was on a plane enroute to Ulithi. After temporary repairs were completed, the *Houston* was ordered to the Brooklyn Navy Yard on the East Coast for permanent repairs. The war was over before repairs were completed.

I reported to the Commanding Officer of the Coronado Base on the 21st as ordered. There were no duties for me to perform. All I had to do was wait for new orders. I was anxious to start my new assignment. I was almost certain it would be my final assignment before the war ended. I did not have long to wait.

On October 29, I was handed orders to report to the LST-343 which was undergoing overhaul at a private shipyard in San Pedro, California, located just a few miles north of Long Beach, California. My orders read that I would be the Engineering Officer of the ship. I knew I would like my new assignment, but I was not so sure about the ship itself.

All I knew about an LST was that it was small, not a combat ship, and used by the Navy to unload troops, trucks, tanks, and supplies on beaches during an invasion.

I reported aboard the 343 on the 29th at night between 11 and 12 PM. As soon as I stepped aboard I knew I was in a different Navy than the one I knew aboard the *Helena* and *Hornet*.

Navy regulations require a guard be posted at the gangway at all times to screen those desiring to come on board. There was no one in sight. A few minutes later a sailor came by. He asked me who I wanted to see. When I told him I was reporting aboard for duty, he said he would try to locate the Officer-of-the-Day.

He had no sooner disappeared through a passageway when the lights went out. Ordinarily when a ship is tied up to a dock, electricity is supplied from connections to shore lines. However, in this instance, they were testing a recently overhauled generating unit which was supplying all the ship's power.

There was complete silence. A few seconds later, I could hear voices, "Turn the lights on! What happened to the lights?" etc. I assumed the man on duty in the generating room would soon switch to another unit and power would be restored. What I didn't know was that no one was on duty. He had left his post and gone ashore.

Approximately fifteen minutes passed. I was standing near the gangway, not knowing what to do, when the Officer-of-the-Day came out with his pajamas on. He told me what had happened. He said since I was the new Engineering Officer possibly I could help restore power.

I was led to the Generating Room. An enlisted man was at work on the faulty unit. The place was a mess with parts everywhere. The parts were from two other generating units which were in various stages of being overhauled. I don't recall what was wrong, but after about an hour of "tinkering", we had the generator running and supplying power again. I had heard of ships with little or no discipline but thought it was all talk. I was soon to learn there was such a Navy.

Shortly after the power was restored, I was taken to a cabin in the Officer's Quarters, located on the main deck under the Bridge. For the first time in my naval career I had my own room.

The room was equipped with two bunk type beds, one over the other. The extra bed was a spare used only when officer personnel passengers were aboard. In addition to the beds, there was a desk, chair, clothes locker, and a small lavatory.

There were ten officers assigned to the ship. Each had his own cabin. The Captain (not a four-striper, but a full lieutenant) had larger and more spacious quarters that included a private bath and shower.

The next morning I toured the ship to take a closer look at my new home. It was not a "fighting" ship although ships of this type were always in the thick of battle during an invasion. The only guns aboard were six 40MM anti-aircraft guns. The ship, obviously smaller than the *Helena* and *Hornet*, was about 300 feet long, 50 feet wide and weighed about 2500 tons.

Most Navy ships have the propulsion machinery and superstructure positioned amidship so that the weight could be evenly distributed fore and aft. An LST is different. The superstructure, all heavy machinery, living quarters for men and Officers, and galley are located in the stern section making the ship ride lower in the stern section than at the bow. The bow section was almost out of the water like an outboard motor boat. With this design, the ship could be steered upon a beach, unload or load and then back away with little difficulty.

The letters "LST" stand for Landing Ship Tank which indicates the primary purpose for which the ship was designed -- to transport Army and Marine tanks and related equipment and personnel to the battle zone and unload them upon a beach during an invasion. We also carried trucks and other vehicles, aviation ground equipment, machinery of every description and personnel to operate the machinery and equipment.

The most unusual feature of an LST is the bow section. The tip of the bow is actually two huge gate-like doors which extend from the main deck to the waterline. These doors could be opened and a ramp inside lowered to load and unload cargo. The cargo area was a huge open space about 30 feet wide by 25 feet high by 200 feet in length.

After seeing the machinery and equipment aboard, it was not hard to understand why the Navy had given me diesel engine training. In addition to the three diesel powered electric generators and two diesel powered boats (LCVPS') the ship's main engines were two huge 12 cylinder diesel engines, the same engines the railroads use to power their diesel locomotives.

For hot water and steam, there was a small boiler. As part of the overhaul, two small electric vaporators were installed by the contractor for the ship's fresh water needs. Prior to this time, they obtained fresh water from shore lines in port and in the war zone their fresh water storage tanks were filled from special fresh water barges.

There was nothing fancy about an LST. They had all the essentials but nothing more. They had a job to do and did it without fanfare. The fighting ships got all the publicity. They had no name, just a number. Like hundreds of other special-purpose Navy ships they were expendable. As evidence, there was no armour plate and no water-tight doors to seal off the various compartments in battle. One well-placed bomb or shell hit would put one out of action or worse.

Notwithstanding the physical limitations there were advantages. The crew consisted of about 120 enlisted men and ten officers. Everyone aboard knew everything there was to know about everybody. We were like a large family. Although the officers had quarters separate and apart from the enlisted men, the rank differential was not as apparent as it was on combat ships.

As a result, enforcement of rules and regulations were very lax. Enlisted men virtually came and went as they pleased. This was due in part from the fact that the ship had just returned from combat duty in the Pacific. After a group of men have fought in battle side by side, rank or rating no longer seem to be important. Everyone on board work together for the benefit of all in combat. Enlisted men follow orders, not necessarily because they wanted to, but it was simply a question of survival. In port, for leave and recreation, was another matter entirely. It was not a time for strict military discipline. It was a time to "eat, drink and be merry."

The contractor, in charge of the overhaul and repair work, was small. Just one of the hundreds of firms who went into business when the war started just to make a "buck". They did not have many skilled personnel. As a result most of the work was sub-contracted. Consequently, there were frequent delays. It was frustrating. They were the most disorganized outfit I ever had to work with.

Most of the officers were married. Naturally, they spent most of their off duty time with their wives living in apartments nearby. The rest of us would head for Long Beach at every opportunity for liberty. On two occasions, we went to Hollywood hoping to meet a few movie stars. We saw many of their homes and favorite night spots, but no stars.

In early December, the overhaul was completed after granting the contractor several extensions to complete his work. After an abbreviated sea trial, we put out to sea heading west. Our destination was Hilo, Hawaii. In less than a week, we were on the beach within walking distance of downtown Hilo.

Hilo is located on the largest island in the Hawaiian chain with a population of about 20,000 at the time. We were there about two weeks loading supplies, equipment, and personnel of a Marine Air Unit for transportation to Roi-Namur Islands in the Central Pacific.

Hilo was too small to be much of a liberty town. There were a few restaurants and night spots, but nothing to brag about. There was one real nice hotel overlooking the waterfront. It was new, but small with less than 50 rooms. They had a real nice restaurant and bar and we would stop by often on liberty for a few drinks.

To my surprise, I heard that one of the largest cattle ranches in the world was located on the island. But the island is better known for having one of the few remaining active volcanoes in the world.

One day several of us borrowed a Jeep from the Marines and toured the crater area. The place was weird-looking with huge craters-no vegetation... with sulphur smoke and fumes pouring from numerous holes and crevices. Although considered dormant at the time, I did not feel comfortable walking through the area. I was glad when we returned to the observation building located at the edge of the crater.

Shortly after the new year (1945) began, we were at sea on our way to the Kwajalein Atoll about 1600 miles west of Hilo. We reached our destination in about one week. Since the top speed of an LST was about 10 knots (12 MPH), we would average some 250 miles during each 24 hour period at sea.

Life aboard an LST was quite a contrast to life aboard the *Helena* or *Hornet*. Part of the difference was my status as an officer as opposed to enlisted status before. But, the big difference was the size of the ship. By comparison I felt I was aboard a row boat. From the Bridge located just above the Officer's quarters, you could see the entire ship from stem to stern.

Because of its size, it did not ride as smoothly as the larger ships. Even the slightest waves would cause the ship to pitch and toss. When the sea became a little rough, the ship would bend in the middle. Yes, I mean bend. Most larger ships have expansion joints which allow the forward and stern sections to move slightly fore or aft in heavy seas without buckling the steel decking. The interaction was so slight aboard the *Helena* that I never noticed it.

But, the movement aboard the 343 was very pronounced. The first time we ran into heavy seas, I thought we would break into two pieces. The mast located just behind the bridge (it extended about 30 feet into the air) would vibrate for about ten seconds after the bow section would bang into a wave ten to 15 feet high. In stormy weather, I kept my life jacket on at all times.

The Wardroom was the center of activities for all of the officers. We ate, played cards or just sat around passing the time of day there. The officers were assigned one mess attendant who took care of our every need... cleaned our cabins, served our food, took care of our laundry, etc.

At mealtime we were treated like a rich plantations owner's family. The table was set with real silver and china. There was even a cloth napkin. To add a little more class, there was a stainless steel napkin ring, with our names on it, around the napkin. The food was not even placed on the table for us to serve ourselves. Instead, the various courses were served separately and individually by the mess attendant.

During the daylight hours at sea, I was kept busy making sure all the machinery was functioning properly. I had about 30 men assigned to my department. Most had been aboard about a year and were experienced in their trade.

While the men were slack in discipline and military bearing, they did their work willingly and cheerfully. More importantly, they knew the machinery and its peculiarities which made my job a lot easier. The main engines gave very little trouble. They would run for hours on end with little or no repairs. The diesel engines driving the electric generators were something else. They were down for repairs most of the time.

We pushed our way onto the beach at Roi-Namur Islands around the first of February. The Kwajalein Atoll is the world's largest carol Atoll. It is composed of a hundred or more islands enclosing a boomerang-shaped lagoon about 70 miles long and 20 miles wide. The landscape was flat like a table top with an elevation of no more than two or three feet above sea level.

Kwajalein, the largest island in the group, was located at one end of the chain of islands with Roi-Namur at the other end. Roi-Namur is really two islands connected by a causeway. They covered an area about two miles long and one mile wide. The only thing of value on the two islands was a Marine Air Base.

Before the war, there was an abundance of trees and vegetation on the island. However, the battle for control of the island on February 1 and 2, 1944, changed the landscape completely. Not a tree could be seen from the beach, only sand remained.

I could not believe that approximately 3500 Japanese troops had been stationed here. Not a Japanese building remained. A Navy Seabee Battalion had completely Americanized the base with Quonset Huts and buildings scattered around the airfield. Someone in describing the scene after the battle for control of the islands one year before said it was a "stinking mess" with debris and dead Japanese scattered over much of the islands. The Japanese lost 7870 men out of 8675 stationed on the island chain. Our dead totaled only 372 out of 41,000 men committed to the battle.

This had been the story of the war in the Pacific beginning with the battle for Kwajalein. American forces were simply overpowering the enemy with men, ships, guns and planes. After leaving the HORNET in June 1944, Saipan fell on June 27th, Tinian on July 31st and Guam on August 12th. We had 5250 men killed in capturing the three islands while the Japanese lost over 24,000 men in the defense of Saipan alone.

The war had entered the desperate stage for the Japanese. The invasion of Leyte on October 20th signaled the return of General McArthur to the Philippines. On February 3, 1945, after bitter fighting, our troops were fighting in the suburbs of Manila. We were pushing closer and closer to the Japanese homeland.

After unloading our cargo, the 343 stayed on the beach awaiting orders to our next assignment. There wasn't much to do except wait. There was a make-shift officer's club no more than 200 yards from the ship. We would go over to the club almost every afternoon for a few drinks and relaxation.

Although our conversation was dominated by the war, our day-to-day activities, and next assignment, we began to talk about our plans after the war. The war in Europe was almost over. The war in the Pacific was in its final stages.

Most of my fellow officers were going back to the job they left when drafted into service. I did not have a job to go back to although it did enter my mind the possibility of getting into the grocery business with Dad. Dad still operated a store at Charleston, but not at the same location.

He had sold the original store along with our home in "downtown" Charleston and moved to Covington in the summer of 1944. Dad explained to Joy and Shirley he did not want them riding the bus to high school. Our new home was located on Sherrod Street (the 200 block) at the southeast corner of Maple Street -- only two blocks from Byars-Hall High School.

He wasn't out of the grocery business long. Within three months, he was back in business. This time, the store was located at the corner of Davis Lane and the Gift-Charleston Road. It remains a mystery to me why he sold out and moved to Covington. Now it was necessary to commute ten miles to and from work each day. Possibly, Mother wanted him out of the grocery business because she had to work in the store most every day with no time to do some of the things she wanted to do.

In any event, I was quite certain I wanted no part of a country store. The work was too confining. All I thought about was getting the war over and away from the Navy. I was quite willing to let the future take care of itself.

On February 19, the Marines landed on Iwo Jima, a volcanic island located about 750 miles east of Tokyo. A few days later, we received orders to load up equipment and supplies for a Marine Fighter Group that was being transferred from Roi-Namur westward. We wondered if it would be Iwo Jima but fully expected it to be much closer to the Japanese homeland.

About one week later, we dropped anchor about ten miles off Saipan where a giant armada was being assembled, not only to back up the invasion at Iwo Jima, but for the next campaign.

While we waited for further orders I had several opportunities to go ashore. There was still some evidence of the death and destruction that had taken place when our forces captured the island. Otherwise, Seabee Construction units had done a tremendous job in rebuilding the roads and buildings necessary to make this a big supply base for our forces in the Pacific. In addition, they had converted the Japanese airfield into one of the largest air facilities in the Pacific. The airfield was being used by our B-29 bombers to blast targets in Japan 1500 miles away (which began in November, 1944). They were the largest planes used in World War II.

While in port, I visited my cousin, Lloyd Davis, from Dallas who was in the Marines aboard a transport awaiting orders to move out. He told me a grisly story of how Marines, after a battle, would knock out the gold teeth of dead Japanese soldiers on the battlefield. I did not believe him until he showed me a small sack of gold teeth.

Around the 20th of March, we received orders to get underway. We were to be part of the invasion forces scheduled to land on Okinawa, just south of the Japanese homeland on April lst. Our particular convoy consisted of about 30 landing ships. There were hundreds of ships (the largest of the war) in the amphibious operation, but we could not see all from our position. Nothing particularly glamorous about a convoy of LST's. No destroyer escort. We were not considered much of a target for the enemy. We just plugged along at 10 miles an hour, hour after hour. We felt relatively safe at sea, but not so sure what to expect when we hit the Hagushi beaches on Okinawa.The voyage was uneventful. I had participated in only one previous invasion (Saipan aboard the *Hornet*). However, on that occasion we were miles away from the landing area and not able to see the action at the landing site.

I was somewhat apprehensive about the invasion. Although, I knew the Japanese would throw everything they had at us and fight for every inch of ground, I was more worried about a new element they had recently introduced into the war -- the Kamikaze pilot.

The Japanese had organized thousands of pilots into a suicide corps whose mission it was to crash their planes into our ships. The planes' gasoline coupled with their bomb load made for an awesome weapon. They had been highly successful during the Battle of Samar in the Philippines and would certainly be used to the fullest at Okinawa.

We did not make the initial landing on L-Day (Sunday, April 1st) as scheduled, but reached the landing site the next day. When we arrived, the sea was a mass of landing craft going to and from the beaches and transports and supply ships anchored off shore. A number of LST's were already in position when we beached in the landing zone. The beach was alive with men and equipment moving toward the battle area.

There was a bluff about 100 feet high, some 300 to 400 yards ahead of our landing position which prevented us from seeing our advancing troops several miles ahead. The men and equipment we carried aboard were destined for Yonton Airfield just beyond the bluff almost directly ahead of our position on the beach.

There was virtually no ground fighting when we arrived. The Japanese had decided not to contest the beaches. Their strategy was to concede the northern portion of the island and concentrate their forces (about 100,000 men) in the southern part where Naha, the islands' capitol, was located.

For a week, there was no real battle ashore as our forces consolidated their easy advances in the north and moved cautiously southward keeping in contact with the main Japanese force.

But, the story at sea was something else. There were daily raids by Japanese planes (primarily Kamikaze) trying to knock out as many ships as possible reinforcing and supplying our troops. My battle station was on the bridge, so I had a front row seat during every raid. I remember the afternoon and evening of April 6th in particular.

On this day, the Japanese committed 355 Kamikaze and 341 conventional planes to the attack. In addition, they sent a Naval force built around the largest ship in the world, the

Yamato (72,908 tons) to wipe out what the Kamikaze pilots left afloat. Our carrier planes (including some from my old ship the *Hornet*) sank the *Yamato*, a cruiser and four destroyers before they reached Okinawa. Only four destroyers made it back to their base at Sasebo, Japan. The sinking of the *Yamato* marked the end of the reign of the battleship as the principle naval vessel afloat. No nation has built a battleship since the end of World War II.

The radar picket ships (primarily destroyers) stationed between 50 and 100 miles from land bore the blunt of the Kamikaze planes heading for Okinawa. The purpose of the picket ships were to warn those of us engaged in landing operations to prepare for an air attack and to pinpoint the incoming planes for our fighter pilots, so they could shoot down as many as possible before they reached their target.

Our main inter-ship communication radio was always set on combat frequencies so we could hear the voice communications from these pickets under attack. It was an eerie feeling listening. In the background, you could hear their guns firing as they reported being under attack. Sometimes you could hear an explosion above the noise of the gunfire. You knew a Kamikaze had crashed into the ship. Sometimes there was silence when the Kamikaze hit the radio section of the ship.

We were ready when the enemy planes reached the landing site. They came in at about 5000 feet heading for the main anchorage where the larger ships were located. I was sure thankful we were a small ship. Our greatest danger was from gunfire from our own ships. A ship next to us was hit by one of our own shells killing three men.

The raid made for a fantastic sight. Hundreds of guns opened up. The exploding shells formed an umbrella overhead. The bursting shell seemed to hold the attacking planes suspended until the pilot nosed the plane over into a dive aiming for his target. I did not see any ships hit in the attack.

The planes either missed their target altogether or were hit several hundred feet above their target and would spin out of control into the water.

Altogether, we lost six ships sunk, ten ships so heavily damaged that they had to be scrapped or out of commission for the remainder of the war, plus seven other ships with damages knocking them out of action for 30 days or more. One of the ships sunk was an LST. Our picket forces sustained most of the losses and damages.

In ten major Kamikaze attacks during the invasion of Okinawa, we lost 34 ships sunk and 66 damaged, most beyond repair. The Japanese lost about 3000 planes during these attacks. The capture of Okinawa cost the Navy 4900 men killed and about 5000 wounded. Most of the deaths and injuries were caused by burns from exploding Kamikaze planes crashing into our ships. What a horrible way to die and what torturing pain the wounded suffered from their burns!

We had unloaded and were about ready to pull away from the beach when a typhoon hit close to the eastern shore of Okinawa. Although we were on the opposite side of the island away from the full force of the storm, we were ordered to stay on the beach. For two days, we bounced up and down like a cork in the heavy seas. Usually, we would come to rest on sand during a landing, but on this occasion the ship lay across a carol reef. After two days of pounding against the reef, we had a sizeable hole in the ship's bottom just forward of the generator compartment.

Fortunately, the hole had penetrated one of our fuel tanks so there was no danger of the ship sinking. However, it did mean that the hole would have to be patched before we could participate in another invasion. When the storm subsided, we got underway and ordered to tow another LST, damaged in the battle, to Pearl Harbor. Instead of our usual speed 10 mph, towing another LST cut our speed in half to 5 mph. Ordinarily we would have arrived in Pearl Harbor two weeks later, but in this situation it took 30 days.

On April 13, we received word that President Roosevelt had died. At the time, everyone was saddened by the news, for we thought he had made a good President and a brilliant leader. Since then, I have concluded that he was not a good President, only a good politician who started this country down the road to becoming a welfare state. While I continue to believe he gave us able leadership during the war, he was partly responsible for us entering the war and most assuredly helped us lose the peace. At the Yalta conference, he gave Russia certain territorial rights which created the Berlin Wall and divided Europe. As a consequence, we see Russia today as an armed camp threatening another global war.

There was a noticeable difference between life aboard an LST at sea as an officer than that of an enlisted man aboard the *Helena* and *Hornet*. For one thing, there was no gambling. Most of the officers liked to play bridge so there was a bridge game in progress every evening after dinner until about midnight. Two officers were real masters of the game and taught us the fine points of bidding, assessing the value of our hand, etc. After a few weeks I learned enough to enjoy the game and played almost every night.

Another source of relaxation was reading. I read a few books aboard the *Helena* and *Hornet*, but very few. Somehow, I never found time to read on the larger ships. For one thing, there were not many books available considering the number of men to be served and, too, the selection was very limited.

About the time I was assigned to the 343, the Navy began to make available large quantities of paperback books. Each month, we would receive a shipment of about 50 books covering a broad range of subjects from fiction to the classics. During this period, I was reading an average of a book every two days. While many were trash, the majority were quality selections by such writers as Hemingway, Bronte, Stephensen,

Kipling, etc. If I had to pick a favorite, it would have to be Rebecca by Daphne du Maurier. The movie by the same title was also top flight.

There were movies, but the big ships like the *Helena* and *Hornet* got all the first-run shows, which left the small ships with re-runs and grade "B" films. Also, our inventory consisted of only two or three different selections, so on a long voyage, movies were not shown very often.

As an enlisted man, in addition to my regular duties, I had a watch assignment (usually four hours on and eight hours off) from the moment we put out to sea. However, as the Engineering Officer aboard the 343, I had no watch assignment, which might explain why I had so much time to read.

The other officers, except the Captain and Executive Officer, rotated in four hour shifts as Officer-of-the-Day on the bridge. Although I knew my responsibilities for keeping the ship's machinery functioning properly was possibly more important than most of my fellow officer's regular duties, I did not feel comfortable about it. Finally, on this trip to Pearl, I asked the Captain to allow me to take my turn on the Bridge with the other officers.

After a brief training period, I was standing the watch alone. Anyone who has ever been in charge of several men at a watch station or had to man a station alone, whether it be in an engineering space, gunnery station, lookout or whatever, knows the feeling of uncertainty connected therewith. One bad decision or failure to do your job properly and the whole ship would be in danger.

None of my previous watch assignments compared with the responsibility of manning the Bridge as O.O.D. This was especially true at night when everyone, except about a dozen men standing watch with me, was asleep. Although I knew the Captain was on call when needed, there were occasions when decisions had to be made on the spur of the moment.

What a lonely feeling knowing the fate of 130 men and the ship was in your hands. It gave me some idea of the tremendous burden the Captain had on his shoulders 24 hours a day. Think of the awesome responsibility the Captain of an Aircraft Carrier with 5000 men aboard must deal with!

On April 30, we heard that Hitler, dictator of Germany, had committed suicide. We knew the end of the war in Europe was at hand. On May 4, the new leader of Germany offered to surrender. On May 8, all the papers were signed by Allied and German leaders and the date is officially designated as V-E Day. We listened by radio to the joyous response by Americans to the news. What a party they had!! From Times Square to San Francisco, from north to south, and in every village, there was dancing in the streets, horns blowing, church bells ringing, the people went wild. Yet, there we were at sea plugging along at five miles per hour toward Pearl Harbor. We were happy too, but knew we still had to finish the war in the Pacific.

The trip to Pearl was not entirely uneventful from an engineering viewpoint. About halfway to our destination, one of our main diesel engines blew a cylinder. With only one engine, we just barely made headway. It took about 24 hours to repair the engine and place it back in operation.

When we entered the channel at Pearl Harbor, the LST we were towing was pushed by a tug to a berth at the Naval Base for repairs. We fully expected to remain at Pearl Harbor also. We were pleasantly surprised when orders were received to report to Seattle, Washington, for repairs.

We arrived in Seattle on or about the 15th of June. Seattle is located on Puget Sound in the middle of a scenic wonderland about 125 miles from the Pacific Ocean. There are mountains all around with one of the highest peaks in the country, Mount Rainier, clearly visible in the distance.

We met with repair supervisors, as soon as we docked, for a conference on the work to be accomplished and to set a tentative time frame for the work to be completed so that leave schedules for the crew could be established.

It was soon evident that there was not the urgency to complete the work in record time as we had anticipated. Instead of what we thought would be no more than a three or four week job, they estimated it would take six to eight weeks, possibly longer. Needless to say this was good news to everyone on board.

Actually, I was hoping the war would be over before repairs were completed. I wanted to end my Navy career in Seattle. I was sick and tired of the war. As it turned out part of my wishes came to pass. The war did end before we left Seattle, but instead of ending my naval career in Seattle, it would end in Tokyo Bay, Japan five months later.

WORLD WAR II ENDS JULY 1945 - FEBRUARY 1946

I liked Seattle. The city did not measure up to San Francisco or Long Beach insofar as night life is concerned. However, they did have an ample supply of cocktail lounges, private clubs, and fine restaurants. I suppose the difference was they catered more to "home folks" than fun-seeking military personnel.

The Executive Officer was a Jewish boy by the name of Lozansky and the only other bachelor officer aboard the 343. We frequently went ashore together. Our first stop on liberty was usually the Athletic Club near downtown Seattle. The purpose of the club was to help its members keep physically trim. However, the only physical fitness program most military men participated in was "elbow-bending" at the bar.

There was a row of 10 to 12 slot machines near the bar. I remember that Lozansky had a "system" in playing these machines. He would put $3 in quarters in the quarter machine and win or lose, quit. It was surprising the number of times he came out ahead. I tried his system, but I almost always lost.

During this period, I went home for a week or ten days. Nothing unusual about my stay in Covington other than the family had moved. They sold their home on Sherrod and purchased a two-story house located one block away at 726 South Main Street.

The house was huge -- two apartments upstairs with the main living quarters downstairs -- and old -- built in the early 1900's. Dad, in later years, referred to the house as the "old barn". This was because of the high ceilings and lack of insulation. It was virtually impossible to heat more than two or three rooms in the winter time. However, it was relatively cool in the summertime, even without air-conditioning.

In late July, known only by a few top advisors and military leaders, President Truman issued a directive authorizing our Armed Forces to use the newly-developed atomic bomb in the war against Japan. On August 6th, an American B29 bomber dropped an atomic device over the city of Hiroshima, Japan, opening a new chapter in warfare. The bomb killed about 80,000 and wounded as many more in this city of about 350,000 population. On August 9th, another bomb was dropped. This time the target was Nagasaki, a city of about 300,000 population. The city was almost totally demolished with virtually 1/2 of the population killed or wounded.

At this point, it was obvious to most of the Japanese leaders that a continuation of the war would be futile. However, there were influential war lords who could not visualize defeat short of complete annihilation.

Had not the Emperor of Japan intervened in favor of peace, it would have been necessary to invade Japan proper resulting in enormous losses on both sides. On August 14th, the Emperor did intervene and agreed to the Allied terms for peace.

I was back in Seattle when the war ended on August 14th. The President declared a two-day holiday. Seattle and the nation went wild, much like they did on V-E day. Again, there was dancing in the streets, church bells ringing, horns blowing -- the works.

I went to downtown Seattle shortly after the news was announced. What a mob! Reminded me of 42nd and Broadway in New York City on New Year's Eve. This was without a doubt the most festive occasion I have ever participated in. The people were deliriously happy -- some crying and laughing at the same time.

Of course, I was in high spirits. I knew it would only be a short time before I would be released from service. The Navy had announced a point system for releasing personnel based primarily upon length of service during the war. Since I had been on active duty since Pearl Harbor, I had accumulated about as many points as anyone in the Navy and would be among the first to be released.

By V-J Day, repairs had been completed on the 343 and we were scheduled to depart several days later. Although our departure date was not changed because of the end of the war, our destination was. Instead of heading back to Okinawa, we were ordered to Sasebo, Japan, which was to be occupied by our forces in early September.

I had mixed feelings about going to Japan. I wanted out, or to be transferred, but I also wanted to visit Japan. Before the war, I had pictured Japan as a good place to spend a vacation. However, now that we had been fighting the Japanese for four years, I wanted not only to see their homeland, but the people that had not only produced the Kamikaze pilot, but soldiers and sailors who would rather die than surrender. We had never fought a war, with any nation, where so few prisoners had been captured.

On the trip west, we stopped off at Saipan to join a convoy of about 15 other LST's enroute to Japan. The voyage was relatively uneventful until we neared Japanese waters. Then we began to sight mines half submerged on the surface of the water.

An underwater mine is a huge ball-shaped device two or three feet in diameter filled with explosives. Spread out over the surface of the mine is approximately two dozen prongs. These prongs are about the same length and twice the diameter of an ordinary lead pencil. Should one of these prongs come in contact with the hull of a ship, the mines explode, which usually means good-bye ship, especially a small ship like an LST.

Ordinarily, this type of mine is anchored to the ocean floor out of sight. They are equipped with a release mechanism, which is triggered when a ship passes on the surface of the water above, allowing the mine to float to the surface striking the ship. However, shortly after our invasion of Okinawa, the Japanese released hundreds to drift in the sea lanes around Japan hoping they would come in contact with some of our ships.

The closer we got to our destination, the more mines we sighted. We posted extra lookouts around the clock. When a mine was sighted our guns would open fire. They would continue firing at the mine until it sank or exploded.

One morning about three days out of Sasebo, I was leaning over the railing just day-dreaming and looking straight down watching the blue water turn foamy white against the side of the ship. The surface of the water was no more than ten feet from where I stood.

I was still looking down when a huge ball-shaped object came into the corner of my vision. It had apparently been in the water for some time, for it was covered with green slime and spotted with patches of rust.

The prongs seemed to be over two feet long: I was terror-stricken and unable to move. I was certain we would hit the mine. As the 343 continued to move ahead, the mine inched closer and closer. By the time it reached my position, it was no more than six inches from the side of the ship. I sensed it was foolish to run so I continued to watch as the mine just barely skimmed by the remaining 25 to 30 feet past the stern of the ship.

I immediately notified the Bridge. They, in turn, notified other ships in the convoy that spotted the mine and maneuvered out of the way. Our guns opened fire. The sea was rough with waves two to three feet high and the mine proved to be a difficult target to hit. After about five minutes of firing, the mine was hit and sank. Possibly it was a dud, but dud or not I was thankful it did not scrape the side of the 343 to know for sure.

We sighted the entrance to the harbor at Sasebo about the middle of September. We were apprehensive about our new assignment. We knew there were several of our warships in the harbor and a detachment of Marines ashore. Nevertheless, we had fought the Japanese for almost four years and could not picture a Jap without a gun or bayonet in his hand. We didn't believe they could be trusted either and expected the fighting to erupt again.

Even the harbor entrance seemed to be saying "keep out". The channel was narrow with rugged 1000-feet plus mountains jutting out of the water on either side shielding the harbor and city from view. Also, the water seemed to be hiding something. The channel had been cleared of mines, but we did not feel at ease until we had cleared the area which had previously been heavily mined.

During the war, Sasebo was one of Japan's principle naval bases. As we entered the harbor and proceeded to our anchorage, it was easy to understand why. The harbor was spacious and well-protected with mountains on virtually all sides. The city of Sasebo itself was located on level ground between the mountains and the harbor.

The first thing I noticed in the harbor was the large number of Japanese Naval vessels. There must have been 25 or 30 in all. Everything from submarines to aircraft carriers. I had pictured them as being sleek and formidable looking. Instead, they looked more like junk.

Some had been bombed by our planes into rusted, twisted shells just barely afloat. Others were in various stages of construction which were discontinued shortly before the war ended. Still others were operational, but antiquated.

Comparing these ships with one of our new cruisers anchored nearby it was difficult to understand how such a motley array of ships could have fought so well and come so close to defeating us in the Pacific.

But these ships were not representative of those we fought in the early days of the war. When the war started, Japan had a modern Navy with some of the finest ships to be found anywhere. As the war progressed, their losses mounted and coupled with our blockade cutting off essential war supplies, they had to improvise causing them to build ships inferior to almost anything we had afloat.

Shortly after we anchored, our Captain reported to the Commandant of our forces in Sasebo for instructions. He returned saying we would remain in the area for several weeks with future orders uncertain. He also reported that there was an epidemic of amoebic dysentery among our personnel in the area. As a result, we were warned not to drink water ashore and avoid coming in contact with the water in the harbor.

The water in the harbor was filthy. Apparently, this city of about 200,000 population, used the harbor as a dump for raw sewage, and garbage of every description. Even though we had evaporators to convert the polluted water into fresh water and treated it with heavy doses of chlorine, I still did not feel comfortable drinking the water.

We were told to be extra careful ashore and only tour the area in groups of two or more. We were also cautioned not to eat ashore. Instead on liberty we carried our own rations and water. In view of all the restrictions, liberty in Sasebo was not very inviting.

During our stay, which lasted four or five weeks, I went ashore two, possibly three times. On my first liberty, Lozansky and I toured the city and surrounding area in a Jeep borrowed from a Marine unit located nearby.

We spent the entire day sightseeing. We had planned to visit Nagasaki about 30 miles away where the second atomic bomb had been dropped. However, we had difficulty in driving over the rough, narrow roads and turned back about 10 miles out of Sasebo.

The Japanese people we saw were cold and indifferent, obviously resenting our presence. On occasions we could hear them talking, but did not have the faintest idea what they were saying. In view of their feelings toward Americans, it was possibly a good thing we didn't understand what they were saying.

The people were shabbily dressed. Their homes were dingy, unpainted frame shacks jammed close together. There was an offensive odor in the air due to the filth in evidence almost everywhere in sight.

I was surprised. I suppose I expected the people and their surroundings to be like some of the Japanese travel posters published before the war. Shortages created by the war could explain the shabby dress and dingy housing, but I do not believe the war could destroy a persons' will to keep clean and live in clean surroundings when water and soap was so plentiful. It was a relief to get back aboard the 343.

Several days later, I received a letter from home saying that a native of Covington was stationed at the Marine Base less than two miles from the 343. We knew each other by sight but, that was about the extent our acquaintance.

A few radio inquiries in the area and we had his location pinpointed. We got together the next afternoon and spent several hours talking about our assignment, home, and the future.

He had a very pleasing personality, easy going, and highly intelligent. I thought to myself, here is a man going places. I was certain he would become, in the years ahead, one of the leading citizens of Tipton County.

His future proved to be entirely different. At this writing (January 1979), with the temperature hovering near ten degrees above zero, he is sleeping in an abandoned unheated house or in his car. He has become a hopeless alcoholic.

His life is ruined. Twenty years ago, he lost a good job because of his drinking problem. Several years later his wife divorced him because of his drinking problem. Following his divorce he lived with his mother. Even though there were frequent alcoholic "binges" he did maintain a certain degree of respectability until his mother died. Since then, he has become little more than a skid row bum.

The last time I saw him, it was evident he had not bathed or shaven in weeks. A friend and I talked about trying to do something for him. We were afraid he would freeze to death. My friend saw him first. He made it clear that he wanted no help from anyone and wanted to be left alone. It makes you wonder what went wrong and if his war experiences had anything to do with his condition.

On October 1, I was promoted to the rank of Lt(jg). No big deal involved. Only a minor change in the uniform insignia and about $20 more salary per month. I was now making over $150 per month.

On October 23, I submitted a request to be discharged from naval service. The request was forwarded to the Bureau of Naval Personnel in Washington for review and approval.

Now the difficult period of waiting began. There was sure to be a four or five week delay before Washington would respond. Even with orders in hand, there could be further delays depending on our assignment and location at the time. Also, there could be delays caused by the availability of transportation back to the States.

During this period, a number of rumors were floating around about our next assignment. One "reliable source" said we would be leaving soon to transport Japanese POW's from Korea to Japan. Another said we would be one of about 100 LST's to be turned over to the Japanese to replace some of the merchant ships they lost during the war.

The last rumor seemed to have substance. In early November, we were ordered to get underway and report to the Tokyo-Yokohama area. The move did not of itself confirm the rumor. However, if a transfer was made, it would most likely be made in the Tokyo area.

I liked the idea of going to Tokyo for a number of reasons. Any assignment would be better than Sasebo. It was an opportunity to see the Capitol and largest city in Japan. But, I was primarily pleased because the Tokyo area was the hub of American transportation activities in the Far East. There, ships and planes were leaving for the United States almost on a daily basis. If and when my discharge papers did arrive, I would not have to wait for transportation back to the States.

The trip to Tokyo was uneventful. The weather was cold. The temperature was well above freezing, but it seemed much colder. There was dampness in the air that seemed to penetrate the heaviest of clothing. This was one trip I regretted volunteering to stand Officer-of-the-Deck watches at sea. After each four hour watch on the open Bridge, I was chilled to the bone.

We dropped anchor several miles from the former Japanese Naval Base at Yokohama. We could see transports, cargo and other larger ships tied up at the dock in the distance. Why LST's were positioned so far out, I do not recall. The principle disadvantage in our location was the 15 to 20 minute motor boat ride each time we wanted to go ashore.

A few days later, several of us went to Tokyo on liberty. We rode the short distance from Yokohama to Tokyo by rail. Our first stop was the downtown business district.

Tokyo at the time had a population of about five to six million. It was a modern city with the usual office buildings, shops, stores, restaurants, etc. One noticeable difference was the absence of tall buildings. The tallest building was no more than ten stories high. Someone said that taller buildings were unsafe because of the high frequency of earthquakes in Japan. In Sasebo, we saw very few Japanese on the streets. In Tokyo, there were hundreds. Most were cleaner and better-dressed than those we saw in Sasebo. There was one very noticeable difference in their appearance. Almost everyone wore a small mask over their nose. Apparently the mask reduced the risk of catching a cold or the flu.

We spent most of the day in the downtown area touring the shops and stores looking for souvenirs. The shops were still feeling the effects of the war and were poorly stocked. I purchased an emerald stone (which mother later made into a ring) and several Kimonos for Joy and Shirley. Before returning to the 343, we went by the Japanese Emperor's palace and General McArthur's headquarters which was located nearby. I was not impressed by the Emperor's palace, primarily because we could not get close enough to see anything. The area was fenced off to keep the public at a distance. Also, trees and shrubbery prevented anyone from seeing much more than the outline of the buildings on the grounds.

By contrast, General McArthur's headquarters was located in a modern office building. At the time and for several years thereafter, the General was in charge of getting Japan back on her feet and establishing a democratic form of government. We had hoped to meet or at least get a glimpse of the General, but he was not in that day. Although very controversial during his lifetime, I believe history will record him as one of our nation's all-time great generals.

Several days later, we borrowed a Jeep and headed for Mount Fuji about 50 miles away. This mountain is a beauty. It is about 12,000 feet high with long gradual slopes and capped in the wintertime with snow. We had planned to take a steam bath and massage at a resort near the base of the mountain but backed out when we got there.

During this period, I was giving much thought to the future. I still wanted to go to college. However, I would not be released from active duty before January or February or possibly March, which would be too late to enter classes during the current school year. So, there would be a waiting period before the September classes began.

It seemed logical for me to remain on active duty, if possible, until August 1946, but not overseas! On December 4, a letter was forwarded to the Bureau of Naval Personnel in

Washington asking for a delay in my request for discharge from naval service and requesting reassignment and duty within the continental United States until August, 1946. While waiting for a reply, we received word that the 343, along with about 100 other ships, would be turned over to the Japanese in January. I did not like the idea of giving the Japanese anything, but realize now it was possibly in our best interest to do so. The war had not only destroyed their Navy, but virtually wiped out their entire merchant fleet as well. Either we had to continue to supply their basic needs with our ships and personnel or turn over some of our surplus cargo type ships so they could take care of their own needs. Now I had something else to worry about. I certainly did not want to be transferred to another ship or station in the Far East before my orders for transfer back to the states were received.

As we waited for the transfer to take place, I went ashore for the last time. On this occasion, we toured an abandoned torpedo manufacturing factory located at the Yokosuka Naval Base. There is a good possibility that the torpedoes which damaged the *Helena* at Pearl Harbor and later sank the *Helena* in Kula Gulf were manufactured there. For souvenirs, I picked up several gyros used to guide the torpedoes and several rifles. I brought one rifle and a gyro home. I still have the rifle but gave the gyro to the science department of the Covington High School.

As luck would have it, three days before Japanese personnel were scheduled to come aboard to take over, I received orders to report to the Commanding Officer of the *U.S.S. Hanover* for transportation to San Francisco for further assignment. Although I was glad not to remain aboard while the Japanese were taking over, I was not happy over leaving my friends from the past 16 months behind. We had experienced some good times and some not so good times together. It was much like leaving home knowing you would not see your family for a long time. At the time, we said we would keep in touch. We had good intentions, but at this writing, I have heard only from one former crew member of the 343. Several years ago, I received a letter from Jack Grist, former supply officer, who resided at the time in St. Petersburg, Florida.

The voyage aboard the *Hanover* was uneventful. We were at sea about 14 days and arrived in San Francisco on February 8. I immediately reported to the Commandant of the Twelfth Naval District. The next day I picked up orders to report to the Eighth Naval District in New Orleans as part of the release from active duty process.

I never did hear from my request to remain on active duty until August. I suppose by the time my request arrived in Washington, orders for release had already been cut. Consequently no action was taken on my request. I was authorized ten days delay in reporting to New Orleans. I boarded a train on the afternoon of the 9th, and arrived in Memphis on the 13th.

The whole family was waiting for me at the depot. What a relief! The remainder of the discharge procedure was anti-climatic. I was home! After all I had been through, I had finally made it home safe and sound.

During the four days at home, I discovered that George and Zack Baddour of Covington and Sam Baddour of Brownsville were taking a vacation in New Orleans. They were leaving by car on the 17th and asked me to come along. We arrived in New Orleans on the 18th.

On the 20th, I picked up orders directing me to proceed to the Naval Air Station at Millington, Tennessee, for processing to civilian status. I arrived in Millington on the 21st. Although my discharge papers indicate a separation date of February 28th, I was processed through the system on the 23rd. I had accumulated five days leave and it was added to the final date making the 28th the official date.

The discharge procedures were not elaborate. There was a physical exam followed by several lectures on benefits available to veterans, and of course, numerous papers to sign.

During one part of the process, we were told to list any and all physical problems we had, as it could have a bearing on any future claims we may have for disability or medical treatment against the federal government. I was currently being treated for stomach cramps which had been giving me problems for the past six to eight months. The doctor said it was caused by the stress and strain of war and should disappear in a few months.

In addition, I was partially deaf to certain tones in my left ear. I had injured the ear off Guadalcanal on the *Helena*. I had fallen asleep under one of our five-inch gun mounts. We were suddenly attacked by several Japanese Dive Bombers. I was still asleep when the guns opened fire. The concussion from the guns caused my ears to "ring" for over a week. Sometime later, I discovered I could not hear certain tones in my left ear.

I listed both conditions for the record. In the event these conditions worsened, I thought the V.A. should bear the expense to correct the problem. Although not my intentions, I must have signed papers applying for disability benefits because a few months later, I received word from the Red Cross office in Covington that the V.A. had denied my claim for disability benefits due to my stomach condition; however, they had approved a 10% disability rating for my ear.

Mrs. C.E. Johnson at the Red Cross office said all I had to do was sign some papers and start receiving a monthly check of about $20 from the V.A. My response was that I had not intended to file a claim, but merely wanted to note these conditions for the record.

I forgot the matter. However, a few weeks later, Mrs. Johnson called again saying I had to do something -- either sign the papers accepting the benefits or send a letter refusing the benefits. I drafted a letter to the V.A. refusing the benefits and the issue was closed. To date, I have not received any further correspondence from the V.A. about the claim.

This was my first experience with disability benefits administered by the federal government. It illustrates how easy it was, and is, to qualify for disability compensation. I was not disabled, yet they had offered me 10%. Thousands upon thousands of veterans and others today under Social Security are drawing disability benefits without any real disability.

Now that I was completely out of the Navy, there was time to reflect upon my years in the military service.

The seven-plus years in the Navy were possibly the most important and surely the most eventful seven years of my life. I had joined the Navy to primarily satisfy a desire to be of service to my country. Call it love of country or patriotism, I was proud to be an American and at the time, service in the military seemed the proper way to express this feeling.

Although the war interfered with my plans to serve four years and then go to college, the war tested this patriotic spirit and proved the feeling was real. In fact, my war experiences seemed to have deepened and strengthened my commitment to preserve the freedom we enjoy in this nation.

It concerns me, at this writing in 1979, that this patriotic spirit which was so much in evidence before, during and immediately after World War II, is so little in evidence today.

Much of the blame for the loss of patriotism is due to our involvement in two no-win wars since the end of World War II. The Korean Conflict and, in particular, the Vietnam War were especially devastating to patriotism in this country. Hundreds of our youth avoided the draft by fleeing to Canada and other countries throughout the world. We pulled out of Vietnam after suffering staggering losses (over 50,000 killed) thereby admitting defeat that further weakened the patriotic spirit in this country.

I was proud of my war-time experiences. I had been tested in battle and proved to myself that I would not panic under fire. I was especially proud of having been able to work my way up through the enlisted ranks to attain commissioned officer status. I will admit there was a lot of luck involved. I happened to be at the right place at the right time. But the miracle of miracles was the fact that I came through all these experiences without a scratch.

My immediate concern was finding a job to tide me over until college started in September. Of course, during the interim I would be staying with mother and dad at 726 South Main Street.

There was a new member of the family. Roy had married Nadine Wilson of the Garland community in April, 1945, and she was living with mother and dad at the time. Roy was still aboard the *Houston* which was operating in the Atlantic helping to clear up the final details of our involvement in the war in Europe. He had several months to run on his six-year enlistment before he would be coming home.

At this point, I had some misgivings about the future because of the uncertainties involved. But, with the war behind me, I, along with every other American, looked forward to the future with great expectations.

THE REST OF THE STORY
YEARS AFTER THE WAR
1946 - 1997

My first job, March 1946, was with a tobacco company traveling over most of west Tennessee and western Kentucky as a sales representative. I married Jean King in December 1946, and then joined a Navy Reserve unit at NAS Millington. I was scheduled to be on active duty one week-end each month and two weeks each summer.

I was recalled to active naval service in January 1951 during the Korean War. Later I was assigned to the Naval Air Station, Atlanta as Assistant Aviation Technical Training officer for week-end reservists. My first daughter, Billie Jean, born in November 1951. Debbie was born in March of 1953. I was discharged from active naval service in January of 1954, and then returned to Covington, Tennessee.

I was assigned to temporary active duty, 60 and 90 day periods (special program…almost full time…off active duty one day…back on active duty the next) as a Recruiting Officer for the Naval Reserve, stationed at the Naval Air Station, Millington until the fall of 1956.

On January first of 1957, I was hired as agent for the State Farm Insurance Company with an office on the west side of the square in Covington. The office moved to the Abernathy Building on West Liberty in 1959.

I was Tipton County chairman of Governor George Wallace's campaign as an American Independent Party candidate for president in 1968. I ran for Congress in the ninth Congressional District as an American Party Candidate in 1969 and placed second in a field of nine.

I ran for Congress in the ninth Congressional District in 1969, and placed second in a field of nine candidates.

In 1969, I ended my military career after 12 years active service and 9 years reserve time.

I was elected to the Tennessee State Senate in 1970, representing Lauderdale, Dyer, Haywood, Crockett, and Tipton counties in West Tennessee, was re-elected in 1974 and again in 1978. I was not able to run for re-election in 1982 due to redistricting. I was the only Independent to serve during those 12 years…no Independents have served in that body since…one of only a few Independents in history to serve in the Tennessee Senate.

By serving as an Independent, I was able to vote my convictions without party politics involved. Another unusual stand was my refusal to accept political contributions over $100. Then there was my stand on Legislative pay. I kept mine less than the lowest paid State employee.

Jean died in March of 1993. I married Helen Oliver in April 1994.

Thursday, November 29, 2001 | THE COMMERCIAL APPEAL

By C. Richard Cotton

Brothers Bill Jim Davis (left) and Rob Roy Davis were stationed together on the USS Helena when it was attacked at Pearl Harbor 60 years ago.

Brothers share Pearl Harbor memories

COVINGTON

By C. Richard Cotton

rcotton4@bellsouth.net

Exactly 60 years ago today, brothers Bill Jim and Rob Roy Davis were peacefully performing routine maintenance on their ship, the USS Helena. A mere eight days later, their world, and most everyone else's, would be forever changed.

The men were like the thousands of other Navy personnel manning ships of all types anchored in the safety of Pearl Harbor. The brothers from Covington had come to accept the routine as their lot in the military of late 1941.

"We really didn't have too much to do," recalled Bill, "but muster and take care of little details that came up."

The light cruiser, designated CL50, was tied to a Pearl Harbor wharf awaiting some time in the dry dock, which was occupied by the battleship USS Pennsylvania. The work on that behemoth was running longer than had been anticipated.

See **PEARL**, NT4

APPENDIX

REMARKS BY STATE SENATOR BILL JIM DAVIS, (I-TN), AT THE *USS HELENA* REUNION, SEATTLE, WASHINGTON, SEPTEMBER 5, 1981.

I am sure each *Helena* survivor feels as I do about the *Helena*. Just the mention of the name, *Helena*, stirs my adrenaline like hearing our national anthem does.

There was something different about the *Helena*. You knew it the instant you reported aboard. Words cannot describe the difference, but whatever it was it made you feel ten feet tall. The difference was reflected in the devotion and dedication of the *Helena* crew which caused them to give their best and more to each and every duty assignment. Other ships had this same spirit, but none with the intensity evidenced on board the *Helena*.

Those *Helena* years produced some of the most enjoyable and fun filled years of our lives -- shore leaves from New York to Buenos Aires, from Long Beach to Honolulu, and from San Francisco to Sydney. Those years also produced some of the most trying, distressing and hazardous times of our lives from Pearl Harbor to Kula Gulf.

We thought it would be a fitting tribute to the *Helena* and be of interest to everyone to briefly retrace and highlight some of the places, events and experiences during those *Helena* years.

Bill Jim Davis

The *Helena*, named for the capitol city of Montana, was commissioned on September 18, 1939, in the Brooklyn Navy Yard just 15 days after World War II started in Europe. Who could forget those liberties in New York City? Why, you could walk any of the streets of New York, day or night, without fear of being assaulted or robbed. There was the World's Fair, Broadway shows, those fabulous movie theatres where on stage they featured some of the top names in show business even the big bands, Glenn Miller, Harry James and all the rest, and other New York attractions too numerous to mention. We saw our first hard evidence of the war during the *Helena's* shakedown cruise to South America in January and February, 1940.

In Buenos Aires, we came in contact with hundreds of German sailors, survivors of the pocket battleship *Graf Spee*. A few days later, we saw the burned out remains of their ship in the Montevideo Harbor. The ship had been scuttled by her crew to avoid destruction by units of the British Navy who were waiting just outside the harbor.

In September, the *Helena* moved through the Panama Canal to the West Coast and on to Pearl Harbor to join the Pacific Fleet. It was a time of testing of the *Helena* and her crew. There were gunnery and training exercises of every description.

By the summer of 1941, Hitler's armies had captured all of Europe with the British standing alone between Hitler and world conquest. Even then, the war seemed remote to most Americans. Nevertheless, we were becoming more and more involved providing England with war materials and other assistance "short of war".

While our attention was focused on the war in Europe, a crisis was developing in the Pacific over a decision by the United States to place an embargo on steel, oil and other war materials destined for Japan who was at war with China.

The embargo set in motion a chain of events which culminated in a decision by the Japanese to strike Pearl Harbor without warning on December 7, 1941, plunging this nation into World War II. Who can forget the surprise and the shock of the torpedo exploding against the side of the *Helena* just before 8 a.m. on that fateful day? Although severely damaged and many of her crew dead and wounded by the sneak attack, the *Helena* quickly recovered. In less than ten minutes, her guns, joined by others in the harbor, drove off the enemy planes with very little additional damage. Captain English placed the day in perspective in a letter dated December 11. Here are four sentences from that letter:

> "The Japanese, while hiding behind a peace mission in Washington, cowardly sneaked the first blow by striking us with bomb and torpedo before the battle was on. In spite of early serious material casualties and the loss of many shipmates, our fire was continuous and decisive. Instances of personal courage are too great to enumerate here. Let it suffice that the *Helena* has definitely won her place in history as a fighting ship which can give it always and take it too when this must be done."

After temporary repairs were made at Pearl Harbor, the *Helena* was ordered back to the States for permanent repairs. Remember the sign near the entrance to the Mare Island Navy Yard? It read, "I don't want to set the world on fire. I just want to start a flame in Tokyo," paraphrasing a popular song of the times. This statement expressed the sentiment of all Americans. We were anxious to carry the fight into the Japanese homeland.

Repairs were completed in late June and the *Helena* headed for the South Pacific where the Japanese were massing their forces for a takeover of the New Hebrides Islands.

We joined our battle forces four days after our Marines landed on Guadalcanal. Remember those dark days? The many hours at battle stations, short rations consisting primarily of dehydrated foods, and those hot tropical days and nights. It was a time when our efforts to stop the Japanese advance hung in the balance. For weeks our forces controlled the area in and around Guadalcanal during the daylight hours and the Japanese at night.

On October 11 and 12, for the first time in the war, the *Helena* Task Force challenged the "Tokyo Express" nightly runs to Guadalcanal. The battle that followed is clearly detailed in Captain Cook's (a *Helena* survivor) fine book, "The Battle of Cape Esperance". This book is required reading for those who are interested in knowing what the war at sea was like in the South Pacific. *Helena's* radar was the first to identify and her guns the first to open fire on the enemy force. Captain Hoover's decision to open fire without specific orders to do so turned almost certain defeat into victory.

Then there was the wild night battle of November 13 and 14. Ours was almost a suicide mission to stop a Japanese super force consisting of two battleships, a cruiser and 14 destroyers from shelling our positions on Guadalcanal. At the very outset of the battle, the *Helena* and the other American ships in column formation, thrust their way between the two battleships firing at times port and starboard simultaneously.

Our losses were heavy. Of the 13 ships entering the battle only one, a destroyer, escaped without a scratch. Two of our cruisers and four destroyers were sunk. The *Helena* received only minor damage with one man killed. But we achieved our goal, turned back the enemy, thereby preventing the heavy attack they had planned on Guadalcanal which would have been disastrous to our Marines ashore and our efforts to stop the Japanese advance.

Of all the accolades we received following the battle, the one I appreciated the most was from the Commanding General of the First Marine Division on Guadalcanal which reads in part, "...but to Scott, Callaghan and their men who, against seemingly hopeless odds, with magnificent courage, made success possible by driving back the first hostile attack, goes our greatest homage. In deepest admiration, the men of Guadalcanal to them lift their battered helmets."

A few days later in Noumea we were shocked and saddened by the transfer of Captain Hoover back to the states. Captain Cecil was ordered aboard as our new skipper.

We participated in two night bombardments on Japanese positions in January. In March, we descended upon Sydney, Australia, for fun and relaxation. What a wild time we had there!

Then it was back to the battle zone for more night bombardments. Finally there was the night of July 5 and 6 in Kula Gulf when we tangled with ten Japanese destroyers. The *Helena* was hit by three torpedoes and sank in three separate sections with 168 shipmates aboard.

Each survivor has a unique story to tell of the ordeal before being rescued. Many, like me, were picked up in the early morning hours by the destroyer *Nicholas* and others by the *Radford*. My brother and some 80 odd other men including Captain Cecil spent the night on a Japanese held island before being rescued by the *Gwin* and *Woodworth*. There were some 200 men at sea on life rafts for two days and nights before landing on Vella Lavella Island. They were cared for by natives and coastwatchers. Nine days later they were rescued by our forces led by the destroyers *Nicholas*, *Radford*, *Jenkins*, and *O'Bannon*.

The *Helena* was the first ship to receive the Navy's Unit Citation Award. She also earned the Asiatic-Pacific Medal with seven battle stars.

Although the *Helena* lies broken and torn, her guns silent, at the bottom of Kula Gulf, her spirit lives on. The spirit lives not only in those of us who were privileged to be a member of her crew but in the annals of Naval history inspiring other ships and crews to hold high the banner of courage and determination in the face of the enemy whatever the circumstances or odds may be.

Won't you join me in a toast to the *Helena* and to those gallant shipmates who gave their lives to make the *Helena* one of the most distinguished fighting ships to sail the seas under the American flag?

"Here's to the *Helena* and to those gallant shipmates who gave their lives in defense of our country. May their memory serve as a reminder of our responsibilities as citizens of this great land to uphold and defend her with all our being including life itself."